# BIRDS,
# BEES AND
# EDUCATED
# FLEAS

After National Service attached to 656 Squadron, RAF, in Malaya, **Bruce Montague** trained at the RADA. In his early twenties, he joined the Old Vic where he appeared in several plays with Vivien Leigh. He has acted in over 300 TV productions but is probably best known for his five-year run in the popular BBC sitcom *Butterflies* as Wendy Craig's would-be lover, Leonard. More recently he returned to the theatre in musicals such as *Fiddler on the Roof* with Topol at the Palladium, *Oliver* (as Mr Brownlow – three years at the Palladium), and *Phantom of the Opera* (two years at Her Majesty's). His latest TV appearance was as a guest star in *New Tricks*. He has written several plays for the theatre and a number of scripts for the BBC, as well as screenplays. Other books include *Wedding Bells and Chimney Sweeps* and *The Book of Royal Useless Information*, which he co-wrote with the late Noel Botham. He lives in Hove and has been married for fifty-two years to the actress Barbara Latham.

The illustrations in this book are woodcuts by the great eighteenth- and nineteenth-century wood-engraver and naturalist Thomas Bewick (1753-1828). Since not all the creatures mentioned in this book were known to science in Bewick's day, the sharp-eyed reader may notice one or two anomalies.

# BIRDS, BEES AND EDUCATED FLEAS

AN A-Z GUIDE TO THE
SEXUAL PREDILECTIONS
OF ANIMALS FROM
AARDVARKS TO ZEBRAS

## BRUCE MONTAGUE

metro

First published by Metro Publishing,
an imprint of
John Blake Publishing Limited
3 Bramber Court, 2 Bramber Road
London W14 9PB

www.johnblakepublishing.co.uk

www.facebook.com/johnblakebooks  
twitter.com/jblakebooks 

First published in paperback in 2015

ISBN: 978-1-78418-010-2

British Library Cataloguing-in-Publication Data:

A catalogue record for this book is available from the British Library.

Design by www.envydesign.co.uk

Printed in Great Britain by CPI Group (UK) Ltd

1 3 5 7 9 10 8 6 4 2

© Text copyright Bruce Montague 2015

The right of Bruce Montague to be identified as the author of this work has been
asserted by him in accordance with the Copyright, Designs and Patents Act 1988.

Papers used by publishing are natural, recyclable products made from
wood grown in sustainable forests. The manufacturing processes conform to the
environmental regulations of the country of origin.

'Let's Do It (Let's Fall in Love)' by Cole Porter.
Copyright © 1928 (renewed) W... Music Corp. (ASCAP)

... has been made to contact the relevant copyright-holders, but some
... We ... appropriate people could contact us.

# Dedication

This book is dedicated to my literary agents, Lesley Pollinger and Tim Bates; to my theatrical agents, Phil Belfield and Mark Ward; to my editor Toby Buchan, and to my publisher, John Blake. Between them they gave me the time, opportunity and encouragement to finish this book, which began over lunch when I asked off-handedly how is it possible for a barnacle to make love. This book is the result of that investigation.

B. M.

*Birds do it, bees do it,*
*Even educated fleas do it ...*
(Lyrics from 'Let's Do It, Let's Fall In Love' by Cole Porter, 1928)

Ah, yes.
But *how* do they do it?
(*Query by the author, 2014*)

# Contents

# Introduction

This is not an academic book. In the words of the great French entomologist, Jean-Henri Fabre (1823–1915), 'Others have reproached me with my style, which has not the solemnity, nay, better, the dryness of the schools.'

I'm sure that serious researchers into animal behaviour will be frustrated by the scarcity of Latin words to describe the biological processes. I've had to use a few because there is no other way to describe certain things. The more obscure words have been given dictionary definitions in the alphabetical index. Perhaps these pages will inspire some curious mind to take a deeper look into these matters and gain fresh insight. The sketch notes that follow are written mainly for laymen like myself.

I absorb interesting trivia like a sponge so, with luck, some of you will share my fascination for curious, extraneous detail.

The seeds of this book germinated when I had one of those random thoughts that strike us all on occasions – how on earth do barnacles breed? They are underwater for the most part, stuck to the bottom of a boat's hull for their entire life, not daring to move, so how do they propagate? (The answer, by the way, is under Chapter 'B'.) Once I had solved the barnacle mystery, my mind wandered further afield. For example, since the primary purpose of sex is to propagate whichever species we belong to, why does a chicken waste her entire life laying unfertilised eggs? (The answer to that is under Chapter 'C'.)

Evolutionary design is blind. All embryos look like fish in the early stages. Why? A billion years ago, the sea reduced in depth, revealing dry land. Some of our ancestors had little choice but to venture onto that inhospitable land and try to survive on it. Animals still start off as fish in the womb before adding and subtracting those bits and pieces that evolution has wrought during an unimaginable length of time. So, in effect, this book has taken millions of years to write.

It seems that in nature nothing happens for a reason. It just happens. Essentially, all animals are the same. It's the differences that make it interesting.

As the French say with saucy insouciance, 'Vive la différence!'

(*Footnote: some of the books to which I owe my research are listed in the Epilogue.*)

BRUCE MONTAGUE

Hove, 2014

## AARDVARK

The aardvark is a nocturnal animal found in sub-Saharan Africa. It has no known relatives, and like the Red Panda (*see Red Pandas*), is the only living species in its order.

Aardvark means earth pig. However it is not remotely related to pigs. To look at, it resembles a bald, hunchbacked rat with the snout of an anteater, but neither is it a rat nor a true anteater. It is not even related to the South American anteater that it superficially resembles. Its unlikely distant cousin, several times removed, is the elephant. Not a kissing cousin though. At full stretch, an aardvark can achieve a length of 6ft, two-thirds of which is tail.

Its big ears move independently, like those of a kangaroo. And if there's a dusty atmosphere, it can somehow button down its ears to keep them clean. It has 20 teeth without enamel or roots called tubulidentata, meaning tube-toothed, which continually regenerate themselves.

The male has a scent gland situated near his testes that emits a strong musky smell. The female has a gland near her vulva, which will emit the appropriate pheromones when her time is ripe.

A shy fellow, the male aardvark only reveals his penis when he is ready for penetrative sex. At this juncture, his penis springs from the prepuce (a layer of skin protecting and concealing the sex organs) and rapidly acquires tumescence. In the Congo, he will mate with many female aardvarks as often as possible between April and May. The gestation period is seven months.

Aardvarks are solitary animals with long extensile tongues and spend their days sleeping deep down in burrows. Their gastronomic delight consists chiefly of termites, though not to the exclusion of other hymenoptera that happen to cross their path. (Hymenoptera is the scientific word for a large order of insects that includes bees, wasps, ants, and sawflies.)

The aardvark is not averse to asserting squatters' rights in old termite nests when ready to give birth. The time of oestrus (the period when most female mammals, except humans, are receptive to sexual activity during which ovulation occurs, commonly called 'on heat') is evident when the area surrounding the female's vagina swells up.

The mother gives birth to a single offspring each season. A baby aardvark weighs less than 4.4lb (2kg) and has smooth pink skin. This little fellow spends his first two weeks in the burrow with his mother, and once he has gained his land legs he will accompany her on nocturnal feeding forays. After 16 weeks, he is completely weaned and at the age of six months he wanders off for a life on his own. Aardvarks have a life span of 10 years in the wild, but can survive twice as long in captivity.

## ALBATROSS

The word albatross derives from the Arabic language and means 'the diver'. The original word described any number of diving birds, including herons. Alcatraz, the island off San Francisco, derives its name from the same root. They were originally called gooney birds and sometimes mollymawks.

When Captain Cook was sailing through Antarctica he came across an island crammed with macaroni penguins, petrels, prions, shearwaters, fulmars and albatrosses. He called it Bird Island. Despite the summers being wet and windy, many birds, including albatrosses, use it as a nesting site. They come here every couple of years to mate and lay an egg. It is possible that their life expectancy could extend to 100 years.

With an 11-ft wing span (340cm), they spend their days cruising over the Southern Ocean and the North Pacific searching for food. They cover almost 1000km every day. Uniquely, they have pipe-like tubes either side of their beaks that act in the same way as pitot tubes on aeroplanes (pitot tubes measure wind velocity). These enable them to judge their airspeed. Albatrosses fly so effortlessly that their heart rate is practically the same when cruising on the thermals as it is at rest. They have the ability to shut down their brain compartmentally, allowing them to fly on auto-pilot so that they can sleep on the wing.

They always build their nests within 72ft (22m) of their previous home or where they were first hatched. They reach sexual maturity at about 5, but generally wait another couple of years before breeding. When courting for the first time they have complex, ritualised dances in which both sexes take part: it is the albatross's way of summing up the suitability of the other bird as a breeding partner. After mating for the first time the pair bond for life.

It takes two years for the great wandering albatross to breed a chick (they lay one egg at a time). For three months they take it in turns to sit on the egg allowing their partner the opportunity to go off and find food. Even after the chickling has hatched, the mother stays with the brood for a further nine months, because in much of their habitat the weather is severely cold. It can take a year before the chick is fully fledged.

Every other year they have regular reunions, which they celebrate by showing off to each other a truncated form of their original courting display as a sort of reassuring gesture.

Widow birds have been known to bond with other females for the purposes of companionship and to assist looking after a chick and, in particular, any orphaned chicks.

## ALLIGATORS AND CROCODILES

Alligators are reptiles (*see Reptiles*). Their native habitat is the eastern section of China, the south of the United States, and along the Gulf coast.

A male alligator is aroused by the scent of musk. He signals sexual desire by immersing himself in the water and practising deep rumbling sounds – so low that humans can barely hear them, but the effects can be witnessed when the water eddies around the reptile and *appears* to start boiling. As in all reptiles, alligators have cloacae, through which they excrete and mate (*see Cloaca*). But the male also has a slight inverted penis.

When the weather is warm enough and their sexual interest is aroused, a male alligator's cloaca will begin to turn inside out and a penis emerges. This he inserts into the receptive cloaca of the female. As with gharials (long-living Indian crocodiles) intercourse takes place in water and usually in early winter so that the eggs can be laid in spring. The female fashions a nest in the sand with twigs and stones where she lays a clutch of about two dozen eggs.

The sex of hatchlings is determined by the temperature of the air during the incubation period. All the baby alligators of one clutch will be of the same sex. The temperature required to produce males must be above 31.7C (89.1F) and below 34.5C (94.1F). This narrow temperature range is so limiting that as a result more females are born than males. The young alligator does not leave home for two years. A male alligator is not sexually mature until he is 10 years old but after that he mates on an annual basis – or as often as the females will let him.

Saltwater crocodiles have been protected in Australia's tropical north since the 1970s. Subsequently, their numbers have increased along with a number of human fatalities.

Like the alligator, a frisky male crocodile disappears underwater and bellows with his mouth closed, causing the water to vibrate and projecting an infrasonic signal to attract receptive females.

When the object of his carnal desire arrives, the crocodile approaches her with a wide mouth. After a perfunctory courtship consisting of head bumping and mutual mooing, the male will attempt to connect sexually. If their relative positions make this too awkward, it has been claimed that the male may take hold of his partner in his mouth and flip her over onto her back before having his way with her in the 'missionary position'. His penis has a fleshy head and a cartilaginous shaft and it protrudes from the wall of his cloaca directly in front of the opening on the belly side. He wastes little time inserting this into her cloaca. It is common for a male to mate any number of times with the same female to ensure her eggs become fertilised. Crocodiles can live to the age of at least 80.

## ANNELIDS (*SEE* WORMS)

## ANTEATERS

Anteaters live in South America. Academics call them edentate animals, meaning they are toothless – a gummy plight they share with sloths and armadillos. There are three subspecies of order Edentata: the giant anteater; the tamandua (smaller, arboreal, collared); the silky or pygmy anteater, the only living species of the genus *Cyclopes* (arboreal, two-toed with big round eyes).

If you were suddenly confronted by a male and a female anteater, it would be difficult to tell them apart. An adult male is 20 per cent bigger than the female but how do you know that you're looking at an adult? The only water they drink is what they can get from the early morning dew and from the ants they eat. Although an anteater has no teeth, it has a tongue that can extend 24in. Its sense of smell is 40 times more sensitive than that of humans.

Their average temperature rarely rises above 91F (32.7C ). They are solitary creatures and extremely docile. They spend 15 hours of every day sleeping. In the wild an anteater waits until he is four years old before he takes up the mating game. He exercises self-control until after the heat of the summer and indulges in copulation only when the females are in the state of oestrus. After a gestation period of approximately 180 days, the female balances herself in an upright position supported by her tail, on the principle that a tripod will not fall over, and then gives birth to a single cub.

As soon as birthing is complete, the youngster climbs onto his mother's back and stays there for a month or so before daring to venture over the side onto solid ground. The cub suckles for six months and does not scout for food independently until about two years old.

## ANTS

Ants and termites: how do you spot the difference? Ants belong to the scientific classification called order Hymenoptera, family Formicidae. They have compound eyes. They can also store formic acid in their bodies that they squirt in self-defence. If this acid hits a human it can incapacitate for hours.

Ants eat anything whereas termites are fussy and confine their dietary requirements to chewing wood and grass. They are also farmers. Over 200 species of ant have evolved to domesticate fungi in the same way as humans farm cows. They milk them, and when the fungi are getting past it, the ants eat them.

Termites belongs to the order Isoptera. Though they are eyeless, rather uncannily they are attracted to the blue end of the spectrum. The most obvious way to tell the difference between an ant and a termite is by examining its life cycle – that is, if you've got the time. An ant goes through a complete metamorphosis, e.g. egg, larva, pupa, adult, whereas a termite doesn't have the pupa stage. It goes from egg to nymph to adult.

A queen termite can lay 11,000,000 eggs every year for up to 15 years. Once the male ant has copulated, like the drone bee, he is doomed to die.

## APES

*'The chimpanzees, in the zoos, do it,*
*Some courageous kangaroos do it...*
(LYRICS BY COLE PORTER)

Monkeys have tails. Apes don't. Barbary apes are not apes at all – they are macaques. There are only 19 species of ape, six of which are the great apes, the rest are gibbons and siamangs. Great apes include bonobos, gorillas, chimpanzees and orang-utans – they are described below, together with the gibbons.

**Bonobos** (pygmy chimpanzees), first discovered in 1929, are among our closest relatives. They share 98 per cent of our genetic profile. In their 1996 book *Demonic Males: Apes and the Origins of Human Violence*, Richard Wrangham and Dale Peterson wrote: 'Chimpanzees and Bonobos both evolved from the same ancestor that gave rise to humans, and yet the Bonobo is one of the most peaceful, unaggressive species of mammals living on the earth today. They have evolved ways to reduce violence that permeate their entire society. They show us that the evolutionary dance of violence is not inexorable.'

The slogan, 'Make love – not war' could have been written by a bonobo, were he to have been given a typewriter, an endless supply of paper and a few million years. To describe these pink-lipped apes with their neatly-parted head of hair as promiscuous

8

is an understatement. Whereas a human may shake hands to say hello, bonobos dispense with the formalities and cut straight to the sex act. If there's a dispute, they resolve it by having sex. If there's a fight, they break off to have sex. If someone does them a favour such as giving them a tasty tit-bit, they respond by... well, you get the idea. No quarrel between a couple of males lasts too long. They soon make up by standing back to back and rubbing their scrotums against each other.

They tongue-kiss, engage in oral sex, and never hesitate if there's the slightest chance of a spot of mutual masturbation. These friendly apes even have a strange 'penis fencing' ritual.

As for the sex act itself, missionaries may have got the idea for their favourite position by observing bonobos and not the other way round. The only taboo for them (bonobos – not missionaries) is sex between a mother and her son. That does not necessarily exclude an Oedipus amongst them somewhere.

The clitoris of the female bonobo is large – three times the size of her human equivalent. It is prominent and waggles provocatively when she walks. Tribadism is common. Tribadism – or 'tribbing' as it is sometimes called – is a form of non-penetrative sex in which two females (ape or human) rub their vulvas together, often, though not exclusively, in the 'scissoring' position. Frottage is similar but involves any part of the body that can be rubbed or stimulated for sexual pleasure. Whatever turns you on, rest assured, the bonobos thought of it first.

The females undergo oestrus for two to three weeks. The gestation period is about 240 days and the babies continue to suckle at their mothers' breasts for up to four years. Baby bonobos, like human tiny tots, are immensely playful. The status of a male bonobo within a troop is dependent on his mother's place in the hierarchy. The male is something of a mother's boy, running to her for protection when in trouble, and remaining bonded to her well into adult life. One theory is that bonobos never fully grow into adulthood, a condition described by learned sociologists as neotony.

**Chimpanzees**: Scientists reckon that approximately five million years ago humans and chimpanzees shared a common ancestor. The DNA of a chimpanzee is nearly 95 per cent identical to that of a human being. The males band together forming close bonds in hunting groups. The same goes with chimpanzees.

They congregate around the Congo River in Africa where their home territories overlap, protected by the females. Like their close cousins the bonobos, chimps can walk upright on two legs when they feel so inclined. The males reach sexual maturity between the ages of 8 and 10, by which time they have developed unusually large testicles. It is suggested that these have evolved due to their polyandrous and highly promiscuous mating habits (*see Polyandry*). Oestrus in females begins at about the age of 10 but they don't become capable of reproducing until after they've reached 13. Then they seldom give birth more than once every four or five years. This slow reproductive rate keeps the population of chimps at a worryingly low level. When a female is in a state of oestrus, her vulva swells for about 10 days, before gradually subsiding. At this time she is in fertile readiness and she makes sure the males know it.

Their nests, which they build in trees, are constructed with twigs and leaves cradling a mattress made of moss. The females take charge of nests, often building two: one for the day and the other in which to sleep at night.

Notwithstanding the fact that a mother chimp does her best to protect her babies, an adult male will kill baby chimps if he is not certain they are his own. To reduce the chance of this happening, the female tends to mate with all the males in the troop, starting with the most dominant of the Lotharios and working her way down to the fumbling novices. By doing this, none of the males can be absolutely sure whether or not he is the father of the baby that is ultimately conceived.

A chimpanzee is a nifty ape. When he makes love, which he does fairly frequently, it only takes a few seconds of his valuable time.

At the time of oestrus, female chimps' genital areas turn pink. The female offers herself from a crouching position and copulation takes place. Within 15 seconds, the male ejaculates. Almost immediately, another male takes his place. This continues until the first male has recovered sufficiently to engage again. This ritual can continue for 10 days.

**Gibbons** are an endangered species of ape. They are monogamous and are fiercely protective of their territory, usually comprising about 25 acres. Small and arboreal, they are tremendous gymnasts, capable of leaping 40ft from one tree to another while travelling at 35mph. This ability to jump great distances between high branches of trees is called brachiating.

When they are on the ground, their preferred manner of travel is by walking upright on two legs just like humans. And they are happy creatures. They sing melodiously, albeit a little eerily.

However, their natural habitat, rainforests, are being destroyed at an estimated rate of 32 acres every minute. Sadly, the rarest mammal in the world is the Hainan gibbon. Running a close second in scarcity is the Eastern Hoolock gibbon.

Gibbons live in nuclear families, and the mother and father sing to each other. They have loud and beautiful voices with a vocal range surpassing human opera singers. Unlike other apes, they don't make nests. On their rumps they have hard cushion-type pads called *ischial callosities* on which they sit in the forks of tree branches.

The female pileated gibbons of Thailand are reputed to have the most beautiful singing voices in the world. The downside to this skill is that it has led to their decline. Their frequent singing alerts poachers as to their whereabouts, and consequently there are fewer than 30,000 pileated gibbons remaining in the wild.

Gibbons become sexually mature at about five years old. They remain with their parents for another three or four years before venturing out to create families of their own. There are so few left today that it takes time for them to find a Mr or Mrs Right.

In New Zealand's Wellington Zoo, Nippy became the longest-living gibbon yet known when he died in 2008 aged 60.

**Gorillas** are the great apes. Polygamous, the family unit consists of a single male (usually a silverback) and his harem. He keeps a wary eye on the females at all times. In all, with wives and infants, a troop can consist of 30 individuals. Another almost constant task for the silverback is to intervene during the squabbling amongst the ladies. When a female comes into oestrus, it is she who initiates the sex act with the silverback. This is performed in a variety of positions including face-to-face on occasions. Over time, he will mate with all the females under his domination. As for his male offspring, he is happy to play with them until they reach the age of six or so, but after that, as he begins to regard them as potential rivals, he gradually loses interest.

The gestation period of gorillas is a couple of weeks shorter than humans. The mothers carry the babies everywhere with them for the first three years. Infant mortality rates amongst gorillas are high because the weakest cubs are often allowed to die. There's no place for stragglers. Another danger presents itself if a stronger male displaces the reigning silverback in battle. The new master may kill the incumbent infants to start breeding his own dynasty.

As young males approach the age of 14, their father drives them out of his troop. He does not care to be threatened by their emerging sexual maturity. Bachelor gorillas go off and form a boys' troop until such time as one of them is overtaken by the desire to start up a family of his own. When he comes across a young female with whom he feels the urge to set up house, he struts around acting tough and beating his chest, King-Kong style. He sniffs her genitals and if she's responsive she will wriggle her hips. After that, one thing leads to another and nature rapidly takes its course.

Gorillas are an endangered species but they are so similar to humans that, in captivity, in order to discover which females are pregnant, human pregnancy kits are used when testing the hormone levels in female gorillas' urine. Female gorillas share the human experience of the menopause, although earlier in their lifecycle: they lose the ability to conceive after the age of 35.

It is a sad fact that gorillas are safer in captivity than they are in the wild where they are ruthlessly hunted by a desperately hungry population.

Mature silverback gorillas are huge (up to 425lb, sometimes even more). But unfortunately for the females, their penis length is in inverse proportion, at just 1.5in (4cm). A silverback lives in a troop of up to 30 females, each one of whom he will mate with throughout the year. There is little competition for females, since a large silverback is scary and easily protects his troop from challengers.

Females mature at 10 to 12 (earlier in captivity); males at 11 to 13. A female's first ovulatory cycle occurs when she is six years old, and is followed by a two-year period of adolescent infertility. The oestrus cycle lasts about a month. Female mountain gorillas are capable of conceiving by the age of 10, and have a cycle of four-year intervals between giving birth. Gorillas mate all the year round.

To encourage her chosen beau to mount her, the female gorilla will maintain eye contact with him while she pouts her lips provocatively. If the male affects nonchalance, she gets irate and slaps the ground; if again this is met with a baleful stare of incomprehension she will go to him and hit him playfully. Before she becomes really upset – and that could mean breaking the furniture – he usually gets the message.

Males incite copulation by approaching a female and displaying before her or by touching her and giving a growly grunt that she realises may lead to tears before bedtime if she doesn't succumb.

Gorillas construct nests of branches and leaves about 2ft to 5ft (0.61 to 1.5m) in diameter and, unlike other great apes, tend to sleep in nests on the ground. The young nest with their mothers, but after the age of three they begin to build their own nests initially close to those of their mothers.

Infants suckle at least once per hour and will sleep with their mothers in the same nest. After five months, the infant apes summon up the courage to break contact occasionally, and by 30 months, only half of their time is spent with mother. Once the offspring are weaned, females begin to ovulate again.

**Orang-utans** are exclusive to Asia. Their native habitat includes the shrinking rainforests of Borneo and Sumatra. The name 'orang-utan' is from Malay *orang hutan* meaning 'man of the forest'. Not only do they have the same number of teeth as humans but they share many of our characteristics. They are even known to mate in the missionary position.

Orang-utans are unique among apes in that they prefer to live a solitary existence. The males avoid each other and keep to their own territory in which they have dominance over several females who, in turn, build their own nests in separate domains. Males are nearly twice as big as females and prefer to roar at each other rather than to fight.

Like humans, female orang-utans have a monthly reproductive cycle, and also like us, there is no outward sign of oestrus. Similarly, gestation is roughly nine months. The female uses sophisticated tools to build her night nests in trees at least 60ft above ground. She goes to bed at 18.00 hours and rises at 06.30. Half of the rest of the time she forages for fruit, honey and insects. Orang-utans are clever and can learn skills quickly. Four hundred years ago, Malaysians even believed these apes could talk but justified the fact that they didn't talk in the presence of humans on their being work-shy.

Infants are dependent on the mother until the age of seven. A female ape becomes capable of giving birth from the age of 14. A male doesn't achieve sexual maturity until about 18.

As with gorillas, the females take the initiative in the mating process; they seek out the strongest. Some adolescent males cannot countenance this and rape has been known to occur among orang-utans. They are like uncivilised humans in many ways.

By 30, the male is a spent-force sexually and when he retires, the heir to the throne takes over. On taking charge, the new fellow doubles in size and weight within a few months.

And now to continue with animals beginning with the letter 'A'.

## APHIDS

Aphids are sap-sucking insects and are known under various names such as greenflies, blackflies, whiteflies and plant lice. They are tiny, varying in length from 0.04in to 0.39in (1 to 10mm) and yet they are a menace to farmers and gardeners the world over. They carry viruses, which they spread from garden to garden.

There are nearly a million species of these insects. What they have in common are their body parts: head, thorax and abdomen together with three pairs of jointed legs, one set of antennae and compound eyes. All insects are cold-blooded.

A *fundatrix* is the founding female of a colony of aphids. Her brood of nymphs will all be female and clonal to their mother. They reproduce rapidly. Mature females give birth to five to ten clones every day. And the clones reproduce more clones. Where are the clones? Don't worry, they're here.

The life expectancy of an aphid is about 30 days, by which time she will be a great-grandmother many times over. Once they have devoured one plant they move on to eat another. This goes on throughout the summer. Some types of aphid reproduce sexually, others are asexual. Some lay eggs, others give birth to live nymphs.

Some species of aphid have the rare ability to produce males through the process of parthenogenesis (conception without fertilisation) as winter approaches. Males and females then reproduce sexually. The female lays eggs that remain dormant through the winter but that will hatch in the spring, beginning another cycle of asexual reproduction.

Ants frequently farm aphids by milking (or stroking) them to obtain their honeydew.

## ARMADILLOS
In Spanish, the word 'armadillo' means 'little armoured one'. Indeed, their leathery shells are constructed in such a way that they appear to be wearing suits of armour. The old Aztec name for them was 'turtle rabbit'. They have sharp claws with which to dig their burrows and to hunt for grubs and other invertebrates.

Depending on the species, gestation takes anything from two months to eight months. They reach maturity within a year of birth. They are nocturnal, solitary animals and do not share their burrows.

The nine-banded armadillo is the largest of the species and weighs as much as 22 lb (10kg). The mating season occurs from

July to August in the Northern Hemisphere and from November to January in the South. Once an egg is fertilised it floats in limbo in the amniotic fluid of the mother (where the foetus stays in a state of suspended animation) until such time as the outside temperature is suitable for gestation to begin. The zygote (a fertilised ovum) then attaches itself to the uterus where it divides into four separate embryos. After four months the quadruplets are born and stay with their mother in her burrow for another three months before venturing out with her on foraging expeditions. Nine-banded armadillos can reproduce once a year for up to 15 years, causing the population of their species to expand rapidly. Only the three-banded armadillo can roll up into a complete ball. Apparently the pheromone of a male armadillo smells like gorgonzola cheese (*see Pheromone*).

## BADGERS

The Romans called them *meles* (the taxonomic name for the genus of badgers) and ate them. The Russians still eat badgers.

Badgers excavate long underground tunnels to live in and these are called setts. In most parts of the world they are solitary animals but British badgers form family clans called *cetes* that contain as many as 15 animals. Grooming plays a major part in their lives. Being nocturnal, their eyesight is poor but they have keen hearing and an acute sense of smell, so it is important for them to share their scent with each other. Males are known as boars, females as sows.

Badgers mate at any time of year but, as in the biology of armadillos, bears and seals, the blastocyst (the cells of an embryo after changes have started to take place) can remain dormant within the womb waiting for external conditions to be just right for the offspring.

The act of mating takes upwards of an hour-and-a-half. The sow delays implantation of the egg until late December through February, the most favourable season for her to give birth. This enables her to correlate with the food supply following weaning. The ability to suspend blastocysts for long periods of time can result in each cub in a litter having a different father.

Newborn cubs are about 12cm long. They live in a specially dug nursery chamber furnished with dry hay, straw and bracken. The sow removes faecal waste and gets rid of it in a designated toilet area outside the sett. Cubs do not open their eyes until they are five weeks old.

Their favourite food includes earthworms, insects and eggs. There are estimated to be about 300,000 badgers in the UK living in 80,000 family groups. The oldest recorded age of a badger is 19.

## BARNACLES

Much to the consternation of sailors the world over, barnacles are crustaceans that stick themselves to the bottom of boats. Their presence slows the speed of the boats by impeding the streamlining. The barnacles stay in one position in that one place for the rest of their lives. Actually, they are hanging upside down with their foreheads stuck to the boat by means of cement glands. They absorb oxygen from the water through their legs – all six of them. They have only one eye that can barely differentiate between light and darkness.

So, how do they mate? The solution is ridiculously simple when you think about it; the barnacle has an inflatable penis that is up to 50 times as long as its body. In fact, it has the longest penis in the animal kingdom, relative to body length.

The penis – up to 24 inches long – once extended, feels around until it comes across another barnacle that has a small hole in the top of its shell. The tactile member inserts itself and the deed is done. The male barnacle has his testes situated near the back of his head and the female barnacle has her ovaries between her head and her legs.

The lady barnacle excretes her fertilised larvae into the water. The *cyprides* larvae (*see Cyprides*) spend what little energy they have left to find a place to rest their weary heads and attach them permanently with a secretion of cement-like substance before metamorphosising into the next generation of baby barnacles stuck to rocks and the hulls of ships.

The word 'barnacle' originated meaning a species of goose. Curiously, our ancient ancestors mistakenly assumed geese developed from barnacles.

## BATS

Bats spend their winters hibernating hanging upside down in roofs and caves. Their metabolic rate is slow to the point of heart-stopping. By February, their body fat has been used up and they need to leave their roost to get a bite to eat and a drop of water. Come March, and they venture out more often but it is not until April that they are hungry enough to go out en masse looking for food. In May, female bats start searching for suitable nursery sites. The males leave them to it and continue to sleep on their own during the day. But at night they go out with their inbuilt sonar devices and collect thousands of insects.

The male Greater Sac-winged bat, native to South America, as the name suggests has sacs attached to his wings into which he mixes a love potion that is irresistible to female bats. This consists of glandular secretions that he scrapes from his penis, which are whisked into his own urine. In late autumn, he flies to the nearest female, and flaps his wings vigorously in front of her. The pheromones given off by his wing-sacs are just too much for a female bat to resist. She will trill in a rather girly way, go to her perch and hang upside down waiting for her lover. He will perch beside her, also upside down. He sidles along until they are touching and being mammals, the rest is just normal upside-down sex.

The cub bat is born with a placenta still attached while the mother continues to hang upside down. The baby clings on tightly and continues to do so even when mother flies off at night listening for moths. Suckling continues for some weeks after the young bat has acquired his own perch in the bats' nursery, which is well organised by a council of mother bats.

The females give birth to a single pup and breast-feed it. By August the young bats are old enough to go out at night and practise their skills at catching moths and suchlike. The crèches disband as the baby bats are weaned off mothers' milk. The adults seek out mating roosts instead. September is the beginning of the mating season. The males will use a variety of noises to attract the opposite sex – whistling and clicking. Consummation takes place and goes on until October. And so their life cycle begins again. Bats just love doing it upside-down. Chandeliers in a cave would represent Bat Heaven. The male climbs onto the back of the female and clings on. This calls for natural acrobatic agility plus a longish penis.

By November, they have stored up enough body fat for another few months of hibernation in caves, barns, trees and belfries.

Incest is rife among horseshoe bats. Grandmothers, granddaughters and any generation in between are happy and willing to consummate their urges with the same male. This results in a lot of in-breeding and a great many kissing cousins.

## BEARS

Bears are solitary animals except during courtship and when rearing cubs. It is a general misconception that they are nocturnal. By nature, they are quadrupeds, though they are perfectly adept at walking and sitting like humans.

There are eight species of bear. Here we take a peek at the North American brown bear, often described as 'the grizzly'. (Polar bears that live in the Arctic and pandas have separate sections of the book to themselves.)

Grizzlies do not reach sexual maturity until five years old. A male grizzly's territory is so extensive it sometimes takes him months to track down a prospective mate.

When courting, grizzlies do a lot of huffing and puffing. The sow may mate in the summer but her reproductive system has an automatic mechanism to delay full implantation of the embryo until it is time to hibernate. In her winter den, the female grizzly (the sow) gives birth every other year to two or three cubs. Often she gives birth while asleep but she is a fiercely protective mother and nurses the cubs for two years.

In China, the territory of black bears overlaps with pandas. The Chinese are fast coming round to protection of the panda, which they now recognise as a valuable asset. On the other hand, the black bear is in a parlous state. These rapidly vanishing animals are the source of bear paws – served up in Chinese restaurants as a potent delicacy. (*See also Polar Bears*)

## BEAVERS

Beavers belong to the order Rodentia. They are nocturnal, semi-aquatic and the second largest rodent in the world. They mate for life but if one of them dies, the survivor will find a new mate. The offspring, known as kits, do not leave the family home until they are two, and both parents share equal responsibility in bringing them up. They build their home, known as 'a lodge', in the calm water behind the dam they've constructed on a stream or river.

Before winter comes, they cover their lodges with a thick mud that quickly sets firm and freezes solid. These lodges usually have two distinct apartments. One is used as a drying-off cupboard when they emerge from water. The other, kept dry, is lined with leaves and is where they actually live. Beavers tails grow huge as winter approaches. They store fat in their tails to live off in the lean winter months. Their hind feet are webbed.

Beavers reach sexual maturity from the age of three. The testes of the male beaver drop to a semi-scrotal position during the mating season and remain enlarged until April. A female will start ovulating about the same time. She excretes on a mound that is maintained exclusively for toilet purposes. The male sniffs this regularly until he is sure ovulation is taking place. In oestrus, the female beaver's nipples grow big and her vulva swells and turns pink in colour. Sexual intercourse takes place from January to February. Litters of up to four babies are born in May and the kits are suckled for three months before being taken out and taught how to forage.

## BEDBUGS

The male bedbug's penis is shaped like a scimitar. Nature has designed his organ thus in order for him to use it as a tool to create a vagina in his prospective mate. The female bedbug is born, and grows up, a total innocent without any sexual orifice. After the male has made his incision and had his way with her, her wound heals, whilst his semen circulates in her bloodstream. Eventually, the semen reaches her ovaries where they fertilise her eggs.

## BEES

Worldwide, there are at least 20,000 species of bee, but only six main types are utilised for commercial honey production: Italian, Caucasian, Russian, German, Carniolan and Buckfast.

In her five-year life, a queen bee makes love for just a few seconds with each of several hundreds of drones specially bred for the task. The queen is selectively bred in a special 'royal bedchamber' and fed royal jelly by worker bees to induce sexual maturity. Before her nuptial flight, the queen kills all potential rival females.

A hive may contain a colony of between 20,000 and 30,000 bees. It is mistakenly believed that bees hibernate in winter. In fact, they create an ecosystem within the hive. They maintain warmth by vibrating their wings at a great rate and they live off their stash of honey.

A worker bee is really a slave. He guards the nursery, he builds the combs, he cleans, scouts and forages. No wonder he rarely lives longer than a month. Drones – male bees – are born to do little else but have sex with the queen. Hundreds of drones will mate with her in mid-air. They are ace fliers and can rotate and fly backwards. After the mating game is over (*see description below*) their *raison d'être* has been fulfilled and they will be starved to death.

The queen lays upwards of 1500 eggs every day. She rules her colony by the subtle emission of her pheromones. She can survive for seven years.

A virgin queen that survives to adulthood without being killed by her rivals will take a mating flight with a dozen or so male drones (out of tens of thousands eligible bachelors in the colony). Being a drone is not conducive to a happy life. Even the poor saps that are chosen to escort the queen on the mating flight don't get lucky. During mating, invariably their genitals explode and snap off inside the queen. Apiarists claim they can sometimes hear the sound of them breaking off. It is little wonder that the male studs are doomed to die. A worker bee will produce one-twelfth of a spoonful of honey during its lifetime. To produce one pound of honey, bees have to tap into 2,000,000 flowers.

It is an irony that the latest pesticides such as neonicotinoids, which protect flora from bugs, are also thought to be responsible for the drastic reduction in the population of honeybees. In January 2013, the European Food Safety Authority concluded that the previous industry-sponsored studies were flawed and that the pesticide posed an unacceptably high risk to bees.

Orchid bees chew orchid flowers, then stuff the resultant cud into their leg pockets. Armed with these attractive pheromones, they fly to their lek, or parading ground, where male orchid bees congregate to demonstrate their acrobatic skills (*see Lek*). They hop, skip, jump, fly and buzz their wings at full fortissimo.

Females gather to watch, like damsels at a joust, and at the end of the demonstration they pick the male of their choice. Then they quietly fly away together for a private fling.

## BEETLES

There are at least half-a-million species of beetle. Certain species get drowsy during the act of copulation to such an extent that they fall asleep. Fortunately, the male's organ remains erect and his partner will finish the job for him.

The favourite habitat of stag beetles is rotting wood where the females lay their eggs that can take as long as seven years to develop into grubs. The remorseless human desire to clean up the countryside is causing a dramatic decline in the numbers of stag beetles as dead wood and rotting vegetation are whisked away.

Fireflies are really beetles, sometimes called lightning bugs. There's a compartment in the abdomen of a firefly that contains a sac of nitric oxide. In the mating season, chemical reactions trigger off the gas to produce quite a bright glow. Magnesium ions, ATP and oxygen react with the enzyme luciferase (distinct from a photoprotein) to produce a 'cold light' with no infrared or ultraviolet frequencies. The flashes of light that come from within the firefly's stomach act as a beacon to female fireflies whose own nitric oxide processes respond. As they seek each other out and gradually get closer to each other, at night the countryside takes on the appearance of being covered in flickering Christmas tree lights.

Within hours of mating, the female firefly lays her eggs in the ground. After about four weeks, the larvae hatch out and feed underground until the end of summer.

There are over 2000 species of firefly and in the larval stages their natural bioluminescence is the reason why they are sometimes referred to as glow-worms.

## BIRDS

*The nightingales, in the dark, do it,*
*Larks, k-razy for a lark, do it...*
(LYRICS BY COLE PORTER)

The sexual organs of birds are called *cloacae*. When birds mate they press their cloacae together. It's quite a quickie. It's called 'the cloacal kiss'. Even so, there are a few types of bird that possess penises, including ostriches and ducks.

Crested **auklets**, seabirds whose territory is around the Bering Sea, have developed a number of characteristics to give them sex appeal. They have a uniquely complex communication system involving songs, visual displays and olfactory signals. Apart from a jazzy trumpet call, they have striking plumage on their crested foreheads and they generate an acidic, fruity smell reminiscent of citrus fruits like lime and lemons.

They begin breeding on the North Pacific coast in June and go on until August, congregating in flocks of a million birds at a time. Mating takes place at sea. The male has no copulatory organ and instead hovers over the female to transfer his seed. Once she is fertilised, the pair remains in a monogamous state for the rest of the breeding year.

**Birds of Paradise** compete to attract mates by means of beauty contests. Such ostentation is a far stretch from their evolutionary roots when they started as ravens and crows.

The New Guinea birds of paradise go through a dancing demonstration and a fashion display unique in the animal world. The male in full regalia sports long springy head ribbons that dangle over his eyes and bob on the ground before him. His breast feathers dazzle with shiny iridescence. His neck droops with beautiful wattles. His overall costume of reds and blues and yellows makes him stand out against the green background of his jungle surroundings.

To begin with, he prepares a bridal path with petals and coloured leaves and plants. Secondly, he struts along this walkway demonstrating his best ballet movements, his feet stepping in a rhythmic yet unpredictable manner. Then, he will suddenly stop and do some subtle Bob Fosse-style manoeuvres. Next, he will shimmy − shaking himself and bobbing his head, feathers and aerials fluttering. This performance is for the benefit of the females who sit bunched up, watching from their overhanging branch in the dress circle.

At the end of the gig, the females will chorus their approval. The dominant female flutters a wing, like a courtesan opening her fan, and the male performer takes up this overt invitation with a whoop of delight. They engage in an enthusiastic coupling that is appraised by the remaining voyeurs with approval and, who can tell, maybe a little envy.

So many birds used to be slaughtered in order to provide fashionable ladies with beautiful plumes to wear in their hats that the numbers of birds of paradise were decimated. Fortunately, today it is illegal to kill one. They are among the few species of animal that is strictly protected. Even so, industrial logging, mining and oil prospecting are fast eroding their habitat.

**Blue jays** mate for life. Come the early spring, any lonely female blue jay that does not yet have a life partner rounds up a group of bachelor males by cajoling them with dancing and singing. The males sit together on a branch of a tree appraising her skills. She takes flight and the males take off and follow her. When she lands, they land. They get together to compare notes and make a lot of noise. Then she takes off again with many of them in hot pursuit, but some are left behind. Every time she lands, the males bob their heads up and down, preening and showing off. At length, she will fly off and only one male will remain. He becomes her partner for life.

After consummation, the male bonds with the female blue jay by feeding her. They start to build nests together. He finds the twigs and she tries to fit them together. After a few false-starts, the pair set up their permanent home in the fork of tree branches, high off the ground. A few weeks later, the hen jay will lay two eggs before she starts sitting to incubate them and then laying another two or three eggs. It takes 17 days for the eggs to hatch and another 21 days before they are fully fledged.

**Bluetits** are not fussy where they live, tending to reside in pipes and letter boxes. The female makes her nest from spiders' webs, leaves and dead grass: the whole lined with down. She lays up to a dozen eggs, timing them to hatch when green caterpillars are in season.

**Bowerbirds** are endemic to New Guinea and Australia. Deep in the woods, male bowerbirds build large houses, or bowers, where they indulge in their courtship rituals, singing and dancing and generally showing off. They tile the floors, place flowers round the walls and litter the vestibule with bright *objets d'art* pinched from all parts of the forest, including shells and debris left over from human waste dumps such as coloured ribbon and pieces of broken glass. If they can find it, the colour they seem to prefer is blue.

Female bowerbirds, their curiosity aroused, cannot resist visiting the exhibitions. They will even taste the paint on the bower walls. As soon as they stop by to appraise the decorative work, they find themselves the object of ravishing male attention. If they approve of the decor, they enter the portals and succumb. Although not naturally monogamous, the female is more likely to choose a male with whom she has mated previously. After they have laid their eggs, the female proceeds to raise her family of chicks without the encumbrance of masculine company.

They use their gift of mimicry as a means of self-protection. Potential predators are fooled into thinking that something other than bowerbirds is around. The birds can faithfully reproduce the snorting of pigs, the chattering of humans and even the cascading sound of waterfalls.

The Australian **brolga cranes** were once called 'The Native Companions'. They bond for life and a feature of a bonded couple is their synchronised call. The female will stand with her beak pointed upward at the sky, her wings folded, and emit a series of bugle calls. Her companion will stand by her side with feathers flared. For every two toots of her bugle, he will blow one longer trumpet response.

Their genetically programmed mating dance is intricate and follows a pattern that seems to be rehearsed. One of the birds will toss a bunch of grass into the air and then leap to catch it in his or her beak. The bird will then leap high into the air and with outstretched wings, stretch its neck, bob its head and strut around as if showing-off. The companion often joins in and they dance together. It has been noted that on occasions a dozen or so cranes line up to face each other and simultaneously perform a kind of square dance.

Male and female cranes that have bonded will share nest-making duties together in the wetlands, whether they are marsh, bog or fen. Single broods of up to three eggs are produced each year, with hatching occurring a month later. Both parents guard the chicks. Should a predator appear, one of the cranes will fly away conspicuously before dropping to the ground pretending to have a broken wing. This distracts the predator sufficiently to lead him away from the nest where the chicks are pre-programmed to lie low until danger has passed.

**Budgerigars** are parrots and they come from Australia. The indigenous people of New South Wales called them 'betcherrygahs' according to the ornithologist, John Gould (1804-1881) who gave them their name in 1840. Sometimes they are called common parakeets and sometimes they are called budgies, but nonetheless they are small, long-tailed, seed-eating birds that are cousins of lories and fig parrots. After the domesticated dog and cat, it is claimed that the budgie is the most popular pet in the world.

Female budgies are bossy birds and somewhat intolerant, whereas male budgies are far more laid back, cheerful, flirtatious and simply love to chat. They have tetra chromatic colour vision, meaning that not only can they distinguish more colours than we can but they also see into part of the ultraviolet spectrum that is invisible to us.

In the wild, budgerigars nest in the hollows of trees, which is why pet budgies need nesting boxes if they are to breed successfully. In Northern Australia, breeding takes place between July and September; in the South they breed later through till January. Budgerigars like to feed each other, particularly their breeding partner. They eat the seeds and then regurgitate them into the beak of their mate. The hen lays up to eight pure white eggs, each on alternate days. Incubation takes three weeks, so there may be as much as a 16-day overlap between the first hatchling and the last. During the whole of this period, the cock bird feeds the mother hen round the clock. However, he is not allowed into the nest until the chicks are hatched.

Male budgerigars have an incredible gift for mimicry. Some people suggest these birds even understand what is being said. Serious scientific studies continue on this subject. An American lady called Camille Jordan had a pet budgie named Puck and according to the *Guinness Book of Records*, Puck could speak 1728 words.

The trill of a male **canary** can thrill a female into immediate submission. His ability to vibrate notes at 16 times per second is too much for a girl to resist. The timing has to be right, of course. He has to time his songs to the lengthening of the day.

There is a wide interest in breeding canaries as cage birds but the fact remains that in the wild, canaries get on with reproduction without any need of human intervention.

Originally, canaries were greenish-grayish-brownish birds. It is only through continual crossbreeding that they have developed into what look like lemons with wings.

The canary is a member of the finch family and has a gregarious nature. Males and females form flocks to forage amongst low vegetation. He hides his nest in a tree or a bush and lines it with feathers and hair. The hen lays clutches of three or four eggs, and two broods per year is the norm. The eggs are bluish-green and take a fortnight to incubate. After another two weeks the chicks are ready to fly the nest.

Male **cockatiels** screech and chirrup and strut to attract the attention of a female. If she is interested in pursuing a relationship she will take a mating stance on a perch. Once they have consummated their relationship they remain bonded for life. Should one of them die, the surviving bird rarely takes another mate.

The Common **Crane**, also known as the Eurasian Crane is the only crane, besides the Demoiselle Crane, that lives in Europe. It will eat almost anything it can get its beak on – from potatoes to worms, from olives to other small birds.

Every spring, a monogamous pair of cranes go through the same courtship ritual. First the male declares his intentions by marching behind the female in a stately way. Then they bow and bob to each other and execute what seem to be ballet steps.

Actually, this is a ritualised dancing display of considerable social significance. The female raises her head and then lowers it as she calls out an enticing scream. The male mimics her and lets out an even longer scream. With luck, copulation follows shortly thereafter.

They build their nests in or near shallow water. They repair this nest and sometimes rebuild it over many years. Should one of the couple die, the widow or widower will attempt to find a new mate.

When nesting, the common cranes wallow in mud in an apparent attempt to blend in with their surroundings. A typical sized clutch is two eggs, laid in May. The incubation period takes about a month during which the pair share baby-sitting duties. The chicks can swim within a couple of hours of hatching and a day later they are capable of running with their parents. They begin to fly after two months. Before the nestlings become fledglings, the parent birds go through a moulting period, rendering them incapable of flight as well as their chicks. This means the entire crane family learns to fly together. A crane reaches sexual maturity at about four years old and its life expectancy is 40 years.

In 2013, the common crane bred in the UK for the first time for 400 years. The population of this once rare bird has now grown to 430,000 across Europe.

The sage **grouse** of North America is also known as Pinnated Grouse (Greater and Lesser Prairie-Chickens) and is an endangered species. From April to May, males flock together on traditional strutting grounds ('lek sites' as they are called) and display their filoplumes and wag their tails to attract females to mate. After copulation, nests are built and hatching takes place in early June. The hen can lay 10 to 12 eggs in a clutch. Related to the grouse are the **ptarmigan** that are found in the arctic regions of North America.

The **bald ibis** became extinct in Europe circa 1750, but it still clings on in Morocco, with a population down to about 500 – that is 2 per cent of what it was 100 years ago.

In the Souss-Massa National Park, together with a smaller colony at Tamri, there were 150 fledglings recorded for the most part of 2013 – a huge improvement thanks to efforts to conserve these vulnerable and weird-looking creatures. They are silent birds except at mating time when they chatter to each other with 'hurrumps' and a call that sounds suspiciously like 'hiya'. Their genus name 'geronticus' is from the Ancient Greek meaning 'old man' for the simple reason that the bald heads of these birds gives them the appearance of old men.

In Morocco, diligent wardens are on hand, constantly monitoring the birds and supplying water for them at times of drought. The recent boost to their population is, to a great extent, due to the efforts of the dedicated conservationists at Birdlife International.

(For anyone who reads this book and is moved, as I am, regarding the fate of some of these beautiful birds, please join Birdlife International, the world's largest partnership of conservation organisations, with over 100 partners, including the RSPB, the Gibraltar Ornithological and Natural History Society, National Audubon Society, Bombay Natural History Society, Birds Australia, Royal Forest and Bird Protection Society of

New Zealand, Nature Seychelles, Malaysian Nature Society and
BirdWatch Ireland.)

**Jacanas** are also called Jesus birds, as they sometimes appear to
be walking on water. They are tropical waders with long, thin
legs and the hen birds are a good 50 per cent heavier than their
male counterparts. Hence, the cocks find themselves somewhat
henpecked.

As a devout feminist, the hen keeps a flock of male jacanas at
her beck and call. Subject to her every whim, the cocks strut and
crow and shimmer their golden wings. From time to time she
selects a mate according to what she considers to be the day's best
display of shimmering. Afterwards, she stands apart, appraising
her male harem aloofly and considers which of them is to be the
next cock to get lucky.

Their nests, put together by the distracted males, are flimsily
built on floating weeds. Passing crocodiles snap up many an egg.
This necessitates the jacana hen to reproduce as often as possible.
While she goes off mating, she leaves the male birds back at the
nest to look after the eggs. The cock has evolved special tuffets
under each of his wings in order to carry chicks. This behaviour
is why, in the early days of ornithology, the male jacana was
mistaken for the hen.

There are two species of **lyrebird** in Australia: the Superb
Lyrebird and Albert's Lyrebird. Like bowerbirds, they possess the
most extraordinary ability for mimicry. They can imitate almost
anything – car alarms, camera shutters, whistles and mewling
babies; even musical instruments like the flute.

They have their own songs too. They can sing with two parts of their voice at the same time and therefore perform duets with themselves. In their courting displays they flaunt their tail feathers, the fronds of which are sinuous and beautifully coloured. These rituals hit their peak during the mating season – from June to August. This is the time when they are at their most vocal. They can live for 30 years.

The mature male **manakin** brings an assistant with him to help him perform his courting display. Perhaps his reason is to prove to the female that his own prowess is better than his apprentice. Or maybe he is timid and needs a Cyrano to woo Roxanne for him. The older male and his junior partner perform whirlies and balancing tricks and a lot of synchronised hopping and singing. Should the female prove sufficiently riveted by this, the mature male dismisses his assistant and continues to bill and coo in his own recognisance.

The **mocking bird** has developed its gift for mimicry into a fine art. It can imitate the cries of almost any other bird. This confuses the competition and the mocking bird remains dominant in his territory. Also they can imitate sounds created by humans, from the ringing of mobile telephones to the clanking of car keys. This uncanny ability is used not only to confuse but it appears to have an added purpose. Female mocking birds are enraptured by such vocal ingenuity and are ready to grant sexual favours to the bird with the widest repertoire.

Female **ravens** will turn homosexual if there are no suitable males around. These girls will even build nests together, move in and share it and snuggle together, although, of course, none of the eggs resulting from their union will be fertilised.

The male Great **Reed Warbler** has a staggering repertoire of tunes. Female reed warblers listen in awe and choose the finest singer of the day to mate with. Chicks of reed warblers with the widest range of notes appear to survive longer, so there is speculation that the more powerful the singer, the stronger is the immune system.

**Robin redbreasts** mate only for as long as is absolutely necessary, after which they fly apart and never squalk to each other again.

House **sparrows** numbers have dropped by 20,000,000 in the past 50 years due to lack of nesting space in new concrete buildings, lack of insects in metropolitan towns and loss of winter feeding in the countryside.

A male sparrow will be paternal to his first mate's brood. If he should have chicks through a liaison with a second hen he will ignore them. This is a dangerous snub. There is no fury like a sparrow scorned. The second, bigamous wife will do her best to kill the chicks of the first legitimate female. Another name for the hedge sparrow is the dunnock. Her average clutch of eggs is five.

**Swallows** and **martins** swoop down and grab their food on the wing. The tail of the male Barn Swallow is nearly 20 per cent longer than that of the hen. This is of considerable importance in the mating season, as a female swallow will always select a mate on the basis of his tail length. The male will choose a nest site and then set about enticing the lady with songs and acrobatic flying. Outside of the breeding season the birds tend to roost in flocks, which can grow to an enormous size. One winter in Nigeria, a roosting site was estimated to contain more than one-and-a-half million birds.

As their name suggests, **weaverbirds** build intricate nests. It's more than a bit of raffia work. The female weaverbird even ties off the ends with neat little knots. Many a male weaverbird learns to his cost that unless his handiwork – or should that be beak-and-claw work – is done with meticulous care, the lady that he is trying to impress will fly off to a more skilful homemaker. When this happens (and it happens more frequently than not) the male has to start again and study his blueprints.

**Wrens** have many varied, complex songs, and sometimes sing duets in harmony. The strange thing is, male wrens pass their songs onto their male offspring. Female wrens pass theirs on to the girls. They are energetic but secretive birds. A great deal more research is being undertaken to understand their lifestyle.

And now to continue with animals beginning with the letter 'B'.

## BISON (EUROPEAN)

Sometimes called *wisent* or the European wood bison, it was thought that this poor beast had been hunted out of existence, the last wild animal having been shot in the North-Western Caucasus in 1927.

However, 54 captive bison were introduced back into the wild and a breeding programme rigidly enforced with the result that today there are more than 5000 wild bison in the forests of Eastern Europe. It is the heaviest land animal in Europe.

One of the major differences between a European bison and its American cousin is that the American fellow has 15 pairs of ribs while the European possesses only 14 pairs.

Bulls become sexually mature at about two years old, but they are prevented from mating in the rutting season by older bulls who like to keep that sort of thing to themselves. So from August to October, one can expect to observe many young, frustrated bulls charging at each other using their horns as weapons. Incidentally, in the middle ages these horns were used as drinking vessels by mediaeval boozers.

A male bison usually gets his first go at mating when he reaches the age of seven, by which time he has grown to a formidable size. Cows have a gestation period of 264 days and typically give birth to a single calf.

## BOAS AND PYTHONS

All boas, if they are to be addressed correctly, are boa constrictors. They are large snakes from the New World and it is a bad idea to upset them by not getting their name right. They tend to come out at night and they have a nasty temper, particularly at the time of year when they have to slough off their skins. They get 'floaters' in their eyes and when they cannot see clearly they will strike out at anything.

They are solitary animals and only get together with another boa constrictor when the urge to mate comes upon them.

They prefer mating in the dry season so the summer months are happier times for boa constrictors. The male can mate with numerous females – they are polygynous (having several female mates) – so August is the time you're most likely to see a smile on his face.

When it comes to breeding time, the female will emit pheromones from her cloaca, summoning males slithering towards her from all directions. During consummation, a male will wrap himself round the female and insert his hemipenes (the sexual organ of a male snake) into her cloaca. Like so many animals, she has the ability to retain the sperm inside her without fertilising her eggs until she senses that the time is ripe. So there is no telling when she will give birth to her baby boa constrictors but when she does the snakelets are born live, wriggling and ready to go.

From the moment of fertilisation, it is estimated that it takes another four months before parturition takes place. The average litter is 25 to 30 little snakes, each averaging 15in to 20in (38cm to 51cm). The babies are independent as soon as they come into the world and they slough their skins regularly every two months as they grow bigger.

Burmese pythons are among the biggest snakes in the world, some growing to a length of nearly 20ft (5.74m). Somehow, they have found their way to the everglades in Southern Florida where they thrive. Their diet includes rabbits, rats and birds. The mothers wrap their own bodies around their brood until the hatchlings employ their 'egg teeth' to cut a hole in the shell to get out. However, worldwide python numbers have been decimated by hunters killing them for their fine, leather-quality skin.

Pythons breed in the early spring and the females lay their eggs in March or April in batches of 12 to 24. As with baby boa constrictors, the newly hatched snakes are soon on their bellies and preparing for their first slough.

## BUGS AND OTHER INSECTS

Jean-Henri Fabre (1823–1915), a French entomologist, devoted his life to the study of bugs, and in the 1870s, he accidentally discovered the importance of pheromones in insects.

One night he was writing in his study and on a table beside him was a cage containing a female peacock moth. It was a lovely evening and the French windows were open. A male peacock moth flew in and sat on the cage. Then another and another until there was a small swarm of male moths. Jean-Henri took these males out into the garden and moved the cage into a back room and turned the lights out.

Later, on his way to bed, he saw that the cage was again covered in male peacock moths. This is when he realised there must be something attracting them to the trapped female. Thus, he began his studies into pheromones. He discovered that the fine and feathery antennae of moths (called *plumose antennae*) have evolved to be attuned to the scents of other moths. And the distillation of the odour can be one in many thousands.

The Giant Silk Moth, the American Cecopria, cannot exist for more than two weeks because it has no mouth or digestive organs. It lives purely to reproduce. When looking for a mate, time is of the essence. Therefore, the female cecopria exudes pheromones so powerful they can attract a male from more than a mile away.

The male bumble bee marks out his hunting territory by flying round from plant to plant marking each with his scent. His search is for sex. He is setting pheromone traps for any passing female. When she lands on one of his marked spaces, he quite literally makes a beeline for her.

Other insects employ visual signals. Butterflies, flies and luminous beetles all use a form of semaphore. Male butterflies are constantly on the lookout for the desired markings on a passing female.

Male flies find an unobstructed space to sit and watch the world go by. They inspect every passing flying object on the off-chance that it might be a female fly. If he sees her, he will escort her like a fighter plane escorting a crippled aircraft to land. They will find a leaf on which to make love.

Fireflies are mentioned elsewhere in this book (page 94) They signal each other by means of a lighting display. Other bugs sing to each other – the chirp of a cricket rubbing its forewings or the cicada's chorus that can easily involve three competing species all calling together. Females thread their way through the cacophony and meet up with like-minded cicadas.

Mole crickets dig burrows with sounding boards built in to make their calls seem louder (*see Cicadas and Crickets*). The head-banging of the death watch beetle as he chews wood is dealt with elsewhere in this book.

## BUTTERFLIES AND MOTHS

*The most refined ladybugs do it,*
*When a gentleman calls,*
*Moths in your rugs do it,*

*What's the use of moth balls?...*
(LYRICS BY COLE PORTER)

Butterflies and moths belong to an order of insects called Lepidoptera. The mating habits of both the butterfly and the moth, though subject to local variations, are pretty similar. Some species, like the European bagworm can reproduce without the need to mate. She is an hermaphrodite. However, parthenogenesis – larvae hatching from unfertilised eggs – is rare.

Most butterflies and moths go through four distinct stages before they flex their wings and soar into the air: egg, caterpillar (or larvae), pupa, adult. Butterflies are generally creatures of the day. Moths go in for night-time activity. Butterflies can detect each other's odour with their antennae. Even though she may be several miles away, a female emitting the right pheromones will attract the attention of a male and he will set out on the long journey to find her. There is a certain time when together, several males trace the scent of a female and flutter towards her en masse. This is called assembling.

As soon as a male gets within hailing distance of the female, he produces a burst of pheromones of his own to let her know he's available. If she is amenable, they go on a short courtship flight where they may consummate in mid-air. Mating can take an hour or so. He finds her egg-laying tube and into it he slips his sperm sac called a spermatophore (*see Spermatophore*).

The female has two sexual cavities; one of these she uses for copulation, the other, called an ovipositor, deposits her 200 or so eggs on the caterpillar food plant she has chosen for her brood.

Butterflies can curve their tongues at extraordinary angles to reach the nectar in flowers. By so doing, they inadvertently collect pollen for the purpose of plant pollination.

Adult butterflies only live for two or three weeks but their life cycle – from egg and through the stages back to egg again – can take over a year. And so the process of regeneration continues: they lay eggs, die and more are born. Come spring, and new generations migrate to the north.

In the US, butterflies spread over the state of New York and even as far as Canada. In the autumn, they flutter south because Red Admirals cannot abide cold weather. They migrate to Georgia and the Carolinas and other deep-south states. This annual phenomenon is mirrored in Europe. Most often on a fine, sunny September day, Red Admirals and – to a lesser degree – Painted Ladies migrate south from the UK to the Mediterranean.

The male and female moths achieve consummation by attaching their abdomens together. He uses little clasps that stick out on either side of his anus to cling onto her. Then he passes a spermatophore sac containing his genes through his penis and into her *bursa copulatrix* – the insect equivalent of a womb. Afterwards, she goes on to have sex with several other moths and stacks their sacs inside her until she is ready to conceive.

Male moth mites are born vivipaparously (being born as a living creature as opposed to coming into the world as an egg). The mites spend their first hours dwelling in their mother's vagina. When a female moth mite gets born, the male moth mite will immediately mate with his sister.

In India and the Far East, Heliothine moths cause around $600,000,000 damage to crops such as lentils and peas every year. Australian scientists are developing a tiny moth penis-inflator called a phalloblaster to identify the destructive types of moth from the harmless varieties. Quite how this will work is a mystery.

Behavioural ecologist, Jess Barber at Boise State University in Idaho discovered that tiger moths generate ultrasonic clicks to startle bats. Bats are the eternal enemy of moths so over the millennia moths have developed a device to thwart the bats' radar.

The moths possess string-like appendages on their abdomens and by flexing and plucking these they can mislead a bat into thinking that the moth smells too awful to eat. Jess Barber has furthered his studies to include hawk moths, which, he claims, generate high-pitched sounds by rubbing their genitals. Apparently, this is enough to discombobulate a bat. It has led to the theory that moths have vibrating penises, which is probably more than enough information to be going on with.

Moth larvae shed their hard outer coating (exoskeletons) half a dozen times before reaching the pupae stage of their cycle.

As if bats aren't dangerous enough for moths, they also have deadly enemies in the form of spiders. There is one food that acts as a Rattlebox moth's defence against spiders. Pyrrolizidine alkaloids are to spiders what garlic is to vampires. If moths ingest enough Pyrrolizidine alkaloids, the pungency of this stuff wafting out of the moth's pores proves anathema to spiders. Certain plants produce Pyrrolizide alkaloids as a natural defence mechanism against insect herbivores. Rattlebox moths get this anti-spider concoction from eating rattlebox plants, hence its name. A female moth doesn't have to eat this particular vegetable. There is enough of this compound in a male's spermatophore when he transfers his sac to the female to make her very presence a turn-off for spiders.

# C

## CAMELS

One hump or two? Bactrian camels, found in eastern Asia, have two humps whereas Arabian camels, better known as dromedaries, have only one. They are mistakenly believed to be cloven-hooved but, in fact, camels are even-toed ungulates. They can live for 50 years. (Llamas, vicunas and alpacas have a family connection with camels but they are not an actual species of camel.)

The Romans formed cavalry units using camels, called *dromedarii*. These were useful in close combat with opposing forces on horseback, because horses are afraid of camels' scent.

Camels are strong and patient but in captivity they are shy. When their hormones are raging, they tend to arrange love trysts in secret places. They do not like to mate while humans watch them.

The male dromedary reaches puberty at about five years old

and continues to have sexual congress in the mating season for another 16 years. The male Bactrian is sexually mature by four years old but his sex life diminishes after the age of 15.

In the wild, the breeding season varies according to the locality. In the Middle East, the rut lasts from October to late April; in the Saharan regions, it goes from October until May; in India, it is from September until March. Preliminaries start with scent-marking. The dromedary crouches to urinate and as he does so, he deliberately splashes his rear quarters. He holds his tail under the anal opening while he sprays. Then he gives four or five beats of his tail to ensure he is well-soaked. He will repeat this procedure throughout the day until his backside becomes dark and thickened with the formation of a mixture of urine and sand.

Unique physical changes take place in a male dromedary as his testosterone levels escalate. He has an active gland called a poll gland on the back of his skull adjacent to the nape of his neck. In the rutting season this gland secretes a thick liquid looking like treacle with a pungent odour that trickles down the sides of his neck. Females are drawn to this like iron filings to a magnet. The process is similar to an elephant in musth (rutting frenzy) when a dark brown liquid exudes from the temples of the elephant's skull.

The male dromedary becomes increasingly aggressive during the rutting season and in a herd will engage in fighting with rivals that can lead to serious injuries. At the same time, another physical change takes place. There is an organ in the mouth of a dromedary called a *dulla* (Arabic) – a large, inflatable sac that protrudes between his lips when in rut. The dulla resembles a swollen tongue hanging out of his mouth. It is not a pretty sight.

To mate, both camels, male and female, sit on the ground, with the male mounting from behind. They are the only ungulates to mate in a sitting position. During copulation, the dulla retracts and he begins foaming at the mouth while he grinds his teeth. The male ejaculates three or four times within a single coupling.

## CATERPILLARS

Butterflies and moths are members of the order Lepidoptera. Caterpillars are butterflies or moths in the larval form. They don't have a sex life because they are *part* of a sex life. They are distinguishable from the larvae of ants, bees and wasps by the absence of nearly all of their front legs, except for the clasper on the extreme end. This forces them to move in a strange humpbacked way as if they are measuring the earth. It is from this loopy, hunchbacked movement that their nickname 'inchworm' arises.

A caterpillar has six stemmata (simple eyes). They eat voraciously and grow so fast they have to shed their skin four or five times before pupating into adult form. Caterpillars of the Monarch butterfly are vividly coloured and would appear to present easy food targets. However, their favourite food is milkweed, a poisonous plant that most animals avoid. Monarch caterpillars have developed immunity to the poison whilst absorbing the toxicity into their systems. The caterpillars have themselves become poisonous, so predators have learned to leave them alone. Even when they transform into brightly coloured Monarch butterflies they retain the poison in their bodies. Would-be predators avoid them.

## CATS

Domestic cats are descended from *Felis silvestris lybica* (African wildcats). The collective noun for a group of cats is a clowder. A male is a tom and a female is a queen. A father cat is a sire and a mother is a dam.

From household pets to the big black panthers, over 80 per cent of cats are turned on by catnip, which contains *nepetalactone*, an oily organic compound that is a mild hallucinogen. It is often collected from tartarian honeysuckle and stuffed into cat toys. It has the opposite effect on certain insects, repelling mosquitoes and cockroaches.

In the course of a year, queens come on heat several times, each period of oestrus lasting about six days. Toms fight over her and the winner will try to mate but the queen will initially reject him. Persistence pays off. At length, she accepts his advances and they mate.

When he withdraws, the queen gives a loud yell of anguish. This is because there are about 150 tiny backward-pointing bristles on the tip of a tom's penis. As he withdraws, the pain of these bristles scraping the edge of her vaginal opening triggers an automatic reaction within the queen to begin ovulation. The act of withdrawal also removes any other tom's sperm that might have been in the queen's vagina.

Following consummation, the queen licks her vulva constantly for about half an hour and will scratch and snarl at any other tom who thinks he can take advantage of her. It is not a certainty that she will start to ovulate at the first act and so she will later mate with other toms. It is often the case that she gives birth to a litter of kittens from different fathers. But frankly, my dear, they don't give a dam.

The average length of gestation is 63 days. On average, four kittens are born – all blind at birth, each weighing 4oz (100gr). They open their eyes after nine days and weaning them off her teats takes the dam (as she is now) another six weeks. They start walking at three weeks... and start scratching the furniture after another four. A cat normally reaches sexual maturity at about six months.

## CATTLE

Placid cows are domesticated fierce, wild oxen. Cattle include cows, oxen and bullocks. They are ruminants. Their digestive systems allow the use of indigestible foods like cellulose by means of regurgitation and chewing the cud. They have stomachs with four chambers: the rumen, the reticulum, the omasum and the abomasum. Each has a different function but the most like a human stomach is the abomasum.

A cow signals she is in a period of oestrus by urinating near the bull who reacts with the flehmen response (a means of identifying and transferring pheromones – *see Flehmen Response under 'F'*). He approaches the cow from behind and rests his head on her rump. If she remains where she stands she is in a state of lordosis, meaning she is willing to be mounted (*see Lordosis under 'L'*).

The gestation period for a cow is nine months. Calving can last anything from three to 72 hours. A newborn calf takes up to half-a-minute before spontaneously breathing. The oldest recorded cow was Big Bertha who died in 1993 aged 48. Cows are colour blind. They cannot distinguish between red and green.

Hindus consider it a mortal sin to kill a cow.

## CENTIPEDES AND MILLIPEDES

It is commonly thought that a centipede has 100 feet. In fact, they may have as few as 20 or as many as 300. They always have an odd number of *pairs* of legs; for example, 19 or 31 pairs – amounting to 38 or 62 legs.

Centipedes do not copulate. The male sets down his spermatophore – his little sac of sperm – and the female will pick it up and stick it somewhere safe. He goes to some lengths to point out where he has deposited it – perhaps on a web or perhaps on a leaf – and he will dance around it to draw it to the female's attention. She is a little slapdash in her arrangements. Having collected several sacs of sperm, she buries them in a hollow and deposits one egg on each sac. She covers up the hole and leaves it alone. The few that hatch and survive become adult centipedes. It can take years for conditions to meet the requirements necessary for a successful hatching. It isn't always wise for a mother to stay around her eggs while they're hatching. Some species of centipede (for example the Scolopendromorpha) eat their mother as soon as they hatch.

## CHAMELEONS

A male chameleon may go to great lengths to impress a lady friend. He'll change colour and pretend to be a bigger fellow than he really is. However, if the lady chameleon is not in the mood, she will glower and her skin will turn dark with red spots. This is her way of saying, 'Not tonight, Napoleon'. Unless he wants a stand-up fight, the wise male chameleon will accept rejection and try his luck elsewhere.

## CHEETAHS

Cheetahs are the fastest animals on earth. They breed at any time of year and mark out their territory with their scent. The female reaches sexual maturity at about two years old. She is lured by the love-call of the dominant male but she needs to be courted by several testosterone-charged males before she can ovulate. Mating can take two days, and the female is only induced to ovulate by performing the sex act.

She gives birth to a litter of blind cubs but they all have their fur markings intact.

After mating she becomes a solitary creature again, except for her cubs of which there may be four or five. These she raises alone until they are 18 months old, at which time she leaves them to their own devices. The cubs form a troop, called a sibling group, and look out for each other for a year or so. Then the females go their separate ways leaving the male cheetahs to bond and hunt as a pack.

## CHICKENS

Humans enjoy sex so much that they frequently go to great lengths to avoid pregnancy. Such behaviour seems unique in the animal kingdom. Replication of the species is the primary purpose of being. So the question is often posed: why do hens lay unfertilised eggs? If a hen had any perception, she would realise that the survival of chickens depends on the insemination of her eggs.

In the wild, chickens instinctively follow this rule. Domesticated chickens aren't the brightest buttons on the beach and are easily cheated by farmers who fool them into thinking their eggs *are* fertilised.

In the nesting sheds, artificial lighting simulates eternal spring and the heating is just right for a broody hen. Once an egg is removed from her nest, the hen is programmed by nature to replace it. And this she does until she is worn out.

Embryos – and human embryos in particular – look like fish in the early stage because we have evolved from the sea. Human embryos develop within the mother and do not need to be incubated in shells. Certain animals (for example the skink) can alternate between bearing live baby skinks and sometimes laying eggs.

The presence of sperm is not necessary to produce an egg but it is necessary to produce a hatchling. So long as there is a cockerel in the vicinity, and the season seems right to the hen, she will continue to lay eggs. The male presence gives rise to the expression, 'ruling the roost'.

The human equivalent of hens laying unfertilised eggs is menstruation – shedding those eggs that are of no further use in the evolutionary process. A human female possesses only a finite number of eggs and once these are used up, the menopause sets in, since there are no more eggs to be 'laid'. And so it is with hens. When she has no more eggs to lay, her time is up, for she is of no more use to her human owners. When cooked they turn out to be tough old birds.

Roosters are kept around on chicken farms to give the hens something to hope for. In fact, one or two breeding hens are also kept to keep the rooster amused. Roosters have the innate capability of always maintaining a reserve tank in their sperm bank. This enables him to mate a different hen every 10 minutes or so without losing energy. In practice, he is not given a wide choice of hen with whom he can get acquainted. Some cockerels preserve their essence by pretending to have sex but holding back on the release of semen, although the hen does not realise it. This is a rare case of a male faking orgasm.

## CICADAS AND CRICKETS

There are three species of cicada that bury themselves and go into hibernation for 17 years, during which time they survive by feeding on xylem (the cells of rotting wood). There are known to be four separate species of cicada that hibernate for 13-year periods.

Up to 30 billion cicadas decide to swarm at the same time. When they eventually emerge – and the temperature has to be exactly right for this to happen, 64F (18C) – the nymphs shed their husks, shake out their new wings, swarm and sing love songs until they find a mate. Only the males sing. After copulation, they live for a further week or so and then die of old age.

A female cicada can lay 400 eggs. A corrugated membrane resonating in the abdomen produces the love-song of the cicada. This is called the tymbal. Their bodies are shaped in such a way as to act as a natural sounding board. The noise of millions of cicadas simultaneously contracting their tymbals produces a dangerously high decibel level. Lady cicadas respond – either through lust or just in an attempt to get the males to shut up – by clicking their wings in a fashion that in cicada circles makes it clear that anyone 'coming hither' will be made welcome. Incidentally, cicadas have five eyes, two of which are most noteworthy for appearing to be bloodshot.

A cricket has ears on its front legs. These ears are membranes of skin that vibrate to sound like timpani. The grasshopper has ears on his abdomen. He sings by rubbing the tiny pegs on the top of his hind legs against his wings.

A randy cricket rubs his wings together producing a chirruping sound that can be irritating to the human ear but to a lady cricket the noise comes across as a flattering and fascinating turn-on. She hurries toward the source of the chirrups, pausing nearby in a seductive pose. He softens his mating call and backs towards her. She climbs onto his back and they stroke each others' antennae. The juices flow. She drinks in his nectar and lowers her abdomen. He raises his abdomen and inserts sperm into her. They repeat this until his juices dry up. Then they part and hop off on their solitary ways.

The female cricket is a promiscuous creature. She mates at least twice a night. To avoid mating twice with the same male, she sprays each of her partners with a warning pheromone that will remind her not to mate with the same individual twice. She doesn't like batting on a sticky cricket.

## CIVETS AND GENETS

These are of the mongoose family and superficially they resemble cats. But they prefer to live in the trees of hot, dense forests. They scuttle up trees rapidly with the use of their tails that make up half their body length. They are creatures of the night.

A typical family group of civets comprises three females and a dominant male. If an outsider invades his territory and makes eyes at any of his harem, the male will fight the intruder to the death. They all make a lot of noise – even when they are not fighting.

They mark out their territory of 250 acres or so by spraying from a scent gland situated on the tip of their anus. They reach sexual maturity when they are two years old and after mating, gestation takes about 70 days for genets and 80 days for the civets. Litters of two or three are the most common. The banded linsang is a Malaysian civet and only eats meat. The African civet is the largest linsang of all – it will eat practically anything.

Civet oil has been used as a perfume base for at least 3000 years and it is alleged to contain medicinal properties that are particularly good for the skin. Synthetic oils have been introduced that replicate the same function as civet oil, but even so the poor creature is being slowly squeezed to death.

## CLITELLUM
The *New Shorter Oxford English Dictionary* gives the following definition of clitellum: 'A raised band encircling the body of oligochaete worms and some leeches, made up of reproductive segments.' (From the Latin, *clitellae* – 'pack-saddles'.)

## CLOACAE
All reptiles, monotremes (egg-laying mammals), amphibians and birds possess cloacae. These are orifices serving as the shared opening for the intestinal, reproductive and urinary tracts. The word 'cloaca' comes from Latin and means 'sewer'. When birds fornicate through these apertures, the act is known among the zoological fraternity as the 'cloacal kiss'.

## COBRAS
The cobra is the world's largest, most venomous snake and a single bite from a king cobra can kill a human being in 15 minutes. It is

unique amongst snakes because it makes a nest for its eggs (20 to 40) on the ground and sits coiled around them until they hatch. The male and female cobras take turns to guard their nest. The incubation period is between 60 and 90 days.

## COCKROACHES

Cockroaches are voracious eaters – they will even resort to cannibalism. Their breeding habits are well documented because they are specially bred as food by lizard fanciers.

There are many types of cockroach but, in most respects, their mating habits are the same. The female uses pheromones to let the males know she is interested. In response the males will practice stridulating (rubbing their legs together pretending they are violins) and standing around puffing themselves out in an attempt to look bigger than they really are.

They mate by standing back-to-back, creating a gentle collision of their respective genitalia. The female develops an egg case called an ootheca capable of carrying up to 40 eggs. She carries this around on her abdomen. When the eggs hatch, they harden and become tiny replications of their parent cockroaches within four hours but it takes three more months before they are fully-fledged. Barring accidents – and lizards – cockroaches can live for as long as four years. A female can produce eight oothecae in her lifetime (about 320 eggs) so they are hardy creatures. Some cockroaches such as *Blaptica Dubia* give birth to live young – these are popular for beetle breeders as food for small reptiles.

## COLLECTIVE NOUNS FOR BIRDS

In general: a flock, flight, congregation or volery. In particular: A watch of nightingales, and the following:

A muster of peacocks
A gaggle of geese (on the ground)
A skein of geese (in flight)
An exultation of larks
A parliament of owls
A charm of finches
A siege of herons, bitterns or cranes
A paddling of ducks
A peep or brood of chickens
A rafter of turkeys
A murder of crows
A chattering of choughs
A covert of coots
A herd of curlews
A cast of hawks
A muster of peacocks
A wing of plovers
A bevy of quails
A building or clamour of rooks
A spring of teals
A fall of woodcock

## COLLECTIVE NOUNS FOR ANIMALS

A crash of rhinoceroses
A rag of colts

# BIRDS, BEES AND EDUCATED FLEAS

A labour of moles
A skulk of foxes
A pace of asses
A cete of badgers
A grist or swarm of bees
A quiver of cobras
A sloth of bears
A sounder of boars
A gang of elks
A fesnyng of ferrets
A skulk of foxes
A husk of hares
A leap of leopards
A troop of monkeys
A yoke of oxen
A kindle of kittens
A clowder of cats
A drift of hogs
A trip of goats
A know of toads
A shrewdness of apes
A troop of kangaroos
A pride of lions
A pod of whales
A school of porpoises
A smack of jellyfish

## CORALS

Corals are single polyps that live in close-knit colonies forming structures such as reefs. Every polyp of coral is a tiny spineless animal that is genetically identical with its companion. There are two methods of reproduction. The first is asexual. The second is by spawning, which involves each polyp releasing huge numbers of gametes simultaneously on the night of a full moon. A gamete is a mature germ cell that unites with another of the opposite sex to form a fertilised ovum. Many corals can only continue to live by the energy given by sunlight. For many years, corals were thought to be plants but at the beginning of the 19th century, William Herschel established they were animals, since they lacked the cell walls characteristic of plants. In the Gulf of Mexico there are certain black corals that live for at least 4,300 years. Their mating habits are so slow, nobody has yet observed what goes on.

## CRABS

The fiddler crab possesses one claw bigger than the other. He waves it enthusiastically until some drab-looking lady crab is sufficiently moved to edge over to see what he wants. Attracting the attention of the opposite sex causes the male crab to change colour, fascinating the female with his versatility and beauty. He invites her to dance and they have a ball. He strokes her legs, she strokes his legs – all eight of them. Then, flushed with excitement, the female will allow herself to be led into the wooer's inner sanctum – a hole in the sand – into which they disappear. What they get up to down there is fairly intimate and eventually results in a whole new generation of crabs.

Californian fiddler crabs are the choosiest creatures. The

females go on a round of inspection of all the available burrows that the males have built before opting for their next honeymoon home, and choosing the architect for their mate.

When they smell the whiff of love pheromones in the water's edge, senior male Japanese Sand Bubbler crabs employ a crafty trick to catch the ladies. They live on the seashore; when the tide goes out they dig deep muddy burrows into the sand and wait patiently indoors while outside, a younger generation of male crabs are falling over themselves chasing females.

To avoid multiple rape, and possibly with becoming modesty, the lady crabs soon head for the freshly dug burrows to lay eggs. The crafty old Brigade of Sand Bubbler crabs hiding inside have anticipated this, so when the girls arrive, the senior sand bubblers grin wisely and agree to hand over their safe havens in return for sex.

Crabs have no ears and yet it has recently been discovered that they are sensitive to sound. It is not known how this works.

## CRAYFISH

American Signal crayfish are larger and much stronger than Britain's only native white-clawed variety, with the consequence that European crayfish are fast facing annihilation. The American aliens also spread 'crayfish plague'. The UK crayfish are freshwater animals and spend the winter in a state of torpor in holes hidden in riverbanks. They mate in late summer through to the end of October. The females excrete pheromones. The sensitive antennules of the males are on the alert and pick up the signals. Their sex organs are situated below the thorax near the front of the abdomen. The males use their abdominal pleopods to transfer sperm into the females' egg sacs.

A female crayfish carries a cluster of fertilised eggs stuck to the underside of her tail throughout the winter months. She is capable of nursing up to 100 eggs that will hatch the following June. European and UK law protect them.

## CROCODILES (*SEE: ALLIGATORS*)

## CRUSTACEANS
A small number of crustaceans are hermaphrodites, but most reproduce sexually. Some change sex during the course of their life. (*See: Barnacles and Lobsters*)

## CYPRIDES
The *New Shorter Oxford English Dictionary* gives the following definition: '...Cirripede larvae at a stage (following the *Nauplius*) in which they acquire shells like that of Cypris ostracods and become anchored to rocks.'

# D

## DEER AND ANTELOPE

In the rutting season, stags can be seen rubbing their antlers against tree trunks or bushes. Within 30 seconds, this unique masturbatory method can produce an ejaculation.

The roebuck will chase a lady deer at top speed so relentlessly that by the time he has caught up with her, they are both too exhausted to perform the sexual act. Sometimes, it takes several chases before he manages to catch her, by which time he still hopes to possess sufficient strength to fulfil his marital obligation.

Antlers are the living symbol of a buck's ability to feed well and look after himself. A mature female will keep an eye open for such signs insofar as they reflect his ability as a good provider. Consequently, female deer succumb more frequently to males with big antlers.

Despite appearances, the North American elk is a kind of

deer although it is not related to the European red deer, nor is it any relation to the moose. Elk gather in herds. The much bigger moose are solitary animals until they can acquire their own harem.

The mating season (known as 'the rut') extends from August until December. A bull defends his harem of around 20 hind against all-comers. He brings the females to heel by bellowing at them in a deafening way that is known as 'bugling'.

A bachelor bull, hoping to get his hooves on the first rung of the sexual stairway of life, struts in front of the reigning patriarch and practices bugling. If neither side is ready to back down, a fight ensues. The weapons of choice are antlers. Antler wrestling easily leads to severe wounding but the winner wins the harem.

To convince the hinds that they have a new master, the winning bull bugles triumphantly while accompanying himself with a long burst of urination. His urinary tract is by nature aimed to shoot up rather than down, enabling him to spray himself with urine all over his belly, chest and legs, which acts as an aphrodisiac to the girls. But he has not finished yet.

The cherry on the cake comes after the bull elk uses his antlers to dig a hole in the mud. He urinates into the hole and rolls in the slush. When he emerges he is caked in foul-smelling mud. From the point of view of the hinds, this is as seductive as a love potion. They literally go weak at the front knees and lower themselves into a submissive, lordosis, position before their new hierarch. The gestation period for a deer is between 200 and 300 days.

Larger antelopes such as dik-diks are monogamous but sometimes form a small herd comprising of two or three females.

Lechwes antelope adopt the lek system (*see Lek under 'L'*)

whereby the males gather on a lekking ground to do a lot of macho showing off. They display their muscles and fight for dominance. The females watch the proceedings closely and eventually the matriarch chooses to mate with the winner.

The biggest antelope, the wildebeest and the impala, form herds with a patriarchal male and a harem of females.

# DOGS

*The world admits bears in pits do it,*
*Even Pekineses at the Ritz do it...*
(LYRICS BY COLE PORTER)

Dogs are descended from wolves that hunt in packs. Domesticated dogs treat their owners as members of the pack. The lifespan of dogs is normally 12 to 15 years.

When golden jackals become a pair they stay faithful to each other for life and cooperate with each other to bring up their family. Foxes are first cousins to dogs (*see 'Foxes'*).

The time it takes dogs to reach sexual maturity depends on their size. For small dogs it is 12 to 18 months old; medium-sized dogs, 15 to 18 months; and large breeds, 18 to 24 months.

When a bitch comes on heat, it lasts for three weeks. In the first stage, her vulva swells and some blood may be discharged. The second stage, after about 10 days, occurs when she is in oestrus. The colour of the discharge turns to a light pink and the area around the vulva softens. The bitch becomes flirtatious and submissive signalling that her ovaries are releasing eggs. By the third week, the discharge will briefly turn bloody again before the flow stops completely. The heat cycle has ended and the bitch has reached what is called the stage of *anoestrus*.

Like most mammals, the male dog's penis is composed of tissue. However, it also contains a small bone thus ensuring virtual certainty of erection. Moments after the dog has mounted the bitch and penetrated her, two glands on either side of his penis will expand inside her vulva. In response, the muscles inside her vulva tighten and clamp so tightly that it is virtually impossible for the dog to release himself from the bitch. They are, in effect, tied together. At this point, he releases his sperm into her canal. They often seem to be in discomfort when they attempt to break apart and finish facing in opposite directions. This can last up to 30 minutes.

The erectile tissue in a dog's penis swells tremendously at the moment of ejaculation, making withdrawal difficult and prolonged, but it also ensures no sperm is allowed to go to waste, which explains why it is sometimes necessary to throw a bucket of water over a pair of coupling canines. Left to their own devices, the swelling will gradually subside and the dogs will separate naturally. The gestation period for dogs varies from 53 to 71 days.

A wolfdog is a canine hybrid produced by the union of a grey wolf and a dog. There are calculated to be over 300,000 wolfdogs in the United States.

Dogs that bite the least include: Beagles, Dalmatians, Golden retrievers, Labrador retrievers, Old English sheepdogs, Pointers, Shetland sheepdogs, Welsh terriers and Yorkshire terriers.

According to the Veterinary Record by Dr Jane Murray and colleagues in the Department of Clinical Veterinary Science at Bristol University, in the year 2011 there were 10,500,000 dogs in the UK. The estimated population of dogs in the USA is 83,300,000.

In the year ending March 2011, 554 Scots were admitted to hospital following dog bites and, in the UK as a whole, there were 6,097 dog-bite cases in casualty departments.

The fifth most frequent cause of visits to emergency rooms in the USA is the result of dog bites, with an estimated 368,000 Americans per year seeking emergency hospital treatment.

## DOLPHINS AND PORPOISES

Dolphins do not achieve sexual maturity until the age of 5. However, they are up for any form of fun and games long before that age. They are eager to explore homosexual encounters as well as masturbation. Homosexual behaviour is part of everyday life for a dolphin, and one particular pleasure for the male is to insert his penis in the blow-hole of another dolphin.

Not only is the penis of a male dolphin retractable, it is a foot long and has a prehensile hook on its tip. This means it can swivel around allowing the male to use his penis to feel for things and for exploration as if it were a hand.

Dolphins have sex on their mind a good deal. They are more than happy to press themselves up to a human, should one be passing by. In fact, it seems that anything that floats past is worth a try from a dolphin's point of view. They have been seen trying to mate with turtles, other large fish and even large balloons. Their taste for sexual intercourse is undiminished by the number of duff encounters they make, but when they do mate, which is often, the act seldom lasts longer than around 15 seconds.

A dolphin's skin is in a state of constant renewal in order to maintain its sleek seaworthiness.

The Ganges river dolphins are peculiar-looking creatures with long beaks and crook-backs. They tend to swim on their sides. However, apart from platypuses, dolphins are the only creatures known to catch their food by detecting the electrical pulses emitted from their unsuspecting prey. They have developed this ability because their eyesight is poor to the point of blindness, whereas platypuses can dimly see but when underwater they keep their eyes shut. The periods December to January and March to May are typically the time when birthing takes place. Gestation is about nine months and the dolphin pups are weaned by the time they are 12 months old. They reach sexual maturity at about 10 years of age.

## DONKEYS AND ASSES

The word 'donkey' was originally pronounced to rhyme with 'monkey', being dun-coloured. Donkeys, horses and zebras are all equine animals. The donkey is the descendant of the African ass, now on the verge of extinction in the wild.

Donkeys have louder voices and bigger ears than horses. It is thought that these have developed because in the desert from whence they came, they had to communicate with each over vast distances. Some donkeys have lived until the age of 60, although generally it is considered that a donkey has had a full life by the time it reaches 40.

A male donkey is called a jack and a female is a jennet. The offspring of a male donkey and a female horse is called a mule and is usually sterile.

When the jennet is in oestrus she often urinates in front of a jack who will react with the flehmen response, before mounting her. The gestation period for a jennet is about a year, and she gives birth to a single foal.

## DRAGONFLIES AND DAMSELFLIES

Dragonflies are insects with two pairs of transparent wings (with the hindwing broader than the forewing) an elongated body and six legs. Even while at rest, the wings are always spread apart. Damselflies, on the other hand, rest their wings together, on both sides of their bodies.

In the spring, it is common to see dragonflies and damselflies swarm. The most likely reason for this is that the males are chasing after females. The majority of male insects have their sperm genitalia at the ninth abdominal segment. Dragonflies and damselflies have back-up genitalia on the second abdominal. Before copulation takes place, sperm is transferred from the first genitalia into the secondary organ.

The large female damselflies of South America mate with a male only when he has convinced her he has created the best potential food site for her to lay her eggs.

Dragonflies copulate whilst flying. The male zooms up and clasps to his bosom the object of his lust. At the end of his abdomen he has special clasps to latch on to his mate, but the clasps work only if the female is of the correct species.

Although they copulate for over an hour, the first half of their union is spent by the male removing previously deposited sperm. He achieves this by twisting his specially barbed penis inside her vagina. If all fits well, she will curl her abdomen forward in order to take possession of his sperm. They spin in the air forming the shape of a heart and this is sometimes known as 'the wheel position'. Following copulation, they frequently remain coupled in flight for half an hour or more. The male probably needs to ensure that no other dragonfly will deposit sperm in his lady's ovipositor.

The lady lays her eggs near water, and when they hatch they are called naiads. Most of a dragonfly's life is spent underwater as a naiad. Naiads have gills in their rectum through which they breathe. They've been known to remain in this state for up to five years. When they leave the water and come up for fresh air for the first time, metamorphosis takes place and they turn into beautiful flying insects, but then their life is nearly over. Adult dragonflies seldom survive longer than 20 weeks.

## DUCKS AND DRAKES

From head to tail, the Argentine Lake Duck measures about 17 inches. The Argentinian Lake Drake has the longest penis of any bird species in the world: his appendage also happens to be 17 inches, what is more, it is shaped like a corkscrew and stretches. The tip of the penis is soft and like a feather duster. The drake employs it to brush away any sperm he encounters that have been deposited by a previous suitor. The vagina of the female duck is ribbed in an anti-clockwise way in order to accommodate the 'screw' of the male. The gestation period for ducks is between three and four weeks.

Kevin McCracken of the University of Alaska conjectures that the randy duck's long penis is an evolutionary adaptation for the males to seem more attractive to the females. What is difficult to understand in terms of evolutionary logic is the reason why drakes employ their legendary length of penis not only for fornication but also to 'lasso' females.

## EAGLES

Eagles are birds of prey, also known as raptors, which is a derivative of the Latin word *raper*, meaning 'to take by force'. They tend to have huge feet with which to carry the animals they kill. Female eagles are generally larger than the males.

Eagles are related to harriers, hawks, kites and vultures. The egg of an eagle is four times as large as a hen's egg. They seldom use their voices. The eye of an eagle is bigger and more clearly focused by far than that of a human

The birds mate for life but every spring they renew their vows by performing courtship dances in the sky. They are superb flyers and can remain airborne for hours.

One of the tricks performed by golden eagles to make an impression on the females is to fly high carrying a rock in their beaks, drop it, then dive at dizzying speed to catch the rock before it hits the ground. Sometimes they will give two or three encores. Females will respond by performing the same trick with something less lethal, such as a twig or a tuft of grass.

Bald eagles have a variation on the courtship ritual. They fly upwards and manouevre like stunt aircraft, with figure-of-eight patterns and cartwheels and sometimes tumbling through the air to catch the talons of each others' feet. This courtship culminates in the two of them settling on a branch or a rock where he mounts her from behind. Copulation takes less than half a minute. Sex is usually of short duration in birds because they only have to adjoin their cloacae for a brief moment to transfer sperm from the male to the female.

The hen lays her eggs (usually a batch of two) 40 to 45 days later. There is a further 42 days of incubation before the nestlings hatch. Although both father and mother sit on the eggs, it is the cock that provides most of the food and feeds the mother. It takes a nerve-racking 37 hours for a chick to break out of an egg. The first chick to hatch invariably eats its sibling.

Eagles tend to use the same nest year after year, and if this isn't possible, they will certainly try to nest in the same location. They share responsibilities for egg-sitting duties that can take many weeks, followed by several more patient weeks until the eaglets are fully fledged. An eagle does not reach sexual maturity until it is 4.

There are no more than 60 pairs of sea eagles left in Scotland due to continual persecution. There is better news regarding the white-tailed eagle. In 1970 it was calculated there were only 2,500 pairs left, while the latest estimate is 10,000 pairs.

## ECHIDNAS

The Echidna is an Australian animal that is not a marsupial but a monotreme, meaning it has only one orifice with which to defecate, urinate and fornicate; in short – a cloaca – just like reptiles and birds.

It has the beak of a bird and lays eggs. It grows spines like a hedgehog and has a marsupial-type pouch. Winter is the time of year that an echidna really looks forward to because that is when it gets round to mating.

Males form an orderly procession behind a female emitting her oestrus pheromones. She walks forward and they follow – sometimes for miles. A couple of weeks later, the female stops to rest and leans her forepaws on a tree trunk while sinking into submissive mode. The males help each other to dig a foot-deep trench around her. Then they have a polite squabble to decide who should be the first man in. If they had invented coins, they would toss for it. The winner sidles into the trench sideways under the female and he presses their cloacae together like a couple of suction pads. It must be a relief to take the weight off his feet.

The female echidna lays her egg three weeks later. From her cloaca emerges an egg the size of a kidney bean. Using several tricky yoga positions, she deposits the egg into her pouch. Two months later the baby's spines begin to develop, causing discomfort in the mother's abdominal area, so the baby echidna is tipped out into the mother's burrow where it has to learn the tricks of an echidna's trade.

## EELS

The fact that eel blood is toxic to humans unless it is extremely well cooked may go some way to explain the steady decline in demand for them in Europe. The symptoms of toxicity are akin to multiple sclerosis. Thus, the population of glass eels, once a delicacy, is in rapid decline.

The life cycle of the European eel was for a long time a mystery. It appeared that nobody had ever discovered a baby eel, and speculation was wildly imaginative as to where they came from. Aristotle was the first person to make a serious observation: he declared they were 'born of earth worms' without the need for fertilisation.

Eels begin their life cycle as transparent larvae called leptocephali. When these were first discovered at the end of the late 19th century, they were not even recognised as anything to do with eels. They feed on marine snow – the minute particles of vegetable jetsam floating in the sea.

In 1922, Professor Johannes Schmidt of Denmark found the smallest eel-larvae ever seen. He had been searching for 20 years and at last scooped them up in the Sargasso Sea, just south of Bermuda. He concluded that this must be the place where eels began their life cycle, although he couldn't prove it at the time. The Sargasso Sea is clogged with berry-like seaweed. The word sargasso is derived from the Portuguese word for grape – 'sargaco'.

However, Professor Schmidt's assumption cannot be verified because nobody has yet discovered how eels actually spawn. No eel has ever been bred in captivity. After spawning (we think) in the Sargasso Sea, eels – or rather their larvae – float with the Gulf Stream across the ocean before reaching the shores of Europe. During the two or three years it takes to get to Europe, they metamorphose into elvers and then into what is called 'glass eels'. They head for rivers where they adapt to fresh water and eat worms and insects. They even slither over dry ground looking for small animals.

After a dozen years – now fully grown and mature – they head back to the ocean and return to the Sargasso Sea. This extraordinary odyssey takes them nearly six months.

We now know there are other spawning grounds including one near Haiti, one off Puerto Rico and yet another north of Antilles, but it remains a mystery how eels find their way home.

## ELEPHANTS

The large African elephants are found on the African savanna. Smaller, Asian elephants are found in the south-east of India. Every day they can get through 250 to 650 pounds of food and drink 50 gallons of water.

A female elephant will court a potential lover for weeks. When she comes into oestrus, she announces her condition by exuding pheromones, which prove beguiling to bull elephants.

A male elephant's sex drive heightens for a couple of months each year when he enters a stage of life called 'musth'. At these times, the bull's testosterone levels rise dramatically and he is prone to violence. He rushes around trumpeting loud mating calls to let all know what an aroused state he is in. Younger males start exuding a pheromone that smells of honey – not to attract the ladies, but rather to reassure their older peer group that they are not yet sexually mature and so do not represent any competition.

During musth, older bulls exude a dark viscous liquid from temporal ducts situated beside their eyes and in front of their ears. This pungent secretion is called temporin and looks like black treacle. It visibly rolls down his cheeks into his mouth, and his violent reaction leaves no doubt that the taste is most unpleasant.

A female elephant goes into oestrus four times in a season every five years. Her gestation period is 22 months. Fortunately they live a long time.

In the off-season, elephants often feel each other up with their trunks. If they sense danger, elephants thump their feet. This resonates for several miles, warning others to be wary.

A herd of elephants comprises up to a dozen adult females with their attendant children led by the matriarch. The mature bulls stay together on the periphery of the herd. Before copulation, a bull rubs the female's vagina and tastes her urine. If she is in oestrus and is agreeable, they will trot off together to make love in private.

When mounted and copulating, the bull elephant does not appear to be making any effort. He does not thrust because he is lucky enough to have a motile penis, which, once in position, does all the work by itself. This is useful since his penis can be as long as 5ft (up to 2m). Afterwards, there is often affectionate post-play. They intertwine their trunks and remain companionable for up to a fortnight before going their separate ways. If the male is still in musth, he may stomp off to find another female.

If the fertilisation is successful, a baby elephant is born 22 months later. For the birthing process, the mother squats down on her haunches and the delivery can take two or three hours. The herd's incumbent aunts and sisters greet the baby by touching him and sniffing him, and they will all contribute to raising him until he is about 14, when he will leave their protection and launch out on his own.

The Duke of Cambridge is President of an organisation called

'Tusk Force'. This attempts to draw the world's attention to the plight of animals and to prevent the senseless poaching of elephants and other African species. It is worthy of the support of all conscientious humans who feel the necessity to protect these helpless creatures. Fuller details are contained in the Epilogue.

In desperation, conservationists are attempting breeding programmes through artificial insemination. With elephants, this has proved to be a particularly difficult process. The semen of most animals can be kept for a certain time in a frozen state to be used for fertilisation as and when necessary. Scientists have not yet been able to successfully preserve elephant semen in cryogenic suspension.

In Africa, poaching has become so serious that a website has been set up to expose not just the killers but also the middle men – the smugglers and the buyers. The site is called Kenyans United Against Poaching (KUAPO) – the 'Poachers Exposed' website. Shaming these cruel and greedy people may not work in an ignorant society. Legislation to enforce sterner measures is desperately needed.

## EMBRYOLOGY

This is a branch of science that deals with the process of development from single-celled zygote to embryo to adult animal. According to the *New Shorter Oxford English Dictionary*, a zygote is: 'A diploid cell resulting from the fusion of two haploid gametes; a fertilised ovum.'

## FISH

*Cold Cape Cod clams, 'gainst their wish, do it*
*Even lazy jellyfish, do it...*

*Electric eels, I might add, do it*
*Though it shocks 'em I know.*
*Why ask if shad do it?*
*Waiter bring me 'shad roe'...*

*Romantic sponges, they say, do it,*
*Oysters, down in Oyster Bay, do it...*

*In shallow shoals, English soles do it.*
*Goldfish, in the privacy, of bowls do it...*
(LYRICS BY COLE PORTER)

**Anglerfish** live two miles beneath the oceans where it's so deep they need a fluorescent beacon that they dangle at the end of a tentacle. This is employed for two reasons: as a lure to arouse the curiosity of passing potential prey and as a signal of their presence to members of the opposite sex. They have two sets of vicious teeth; one set is in their jaws, the other is in the back of their throat. Once you're behind the first set of gnashers there's no escape.

Many times smaller than the female of his species, the male anglerfish does nothing. His huge mouth with its needle-length teeth is always open but apart from that, he floats in the water in a state of near-stupefaction. By the time he is sexually mature his digestive system shuts down so that he can no longer eat. To survive and, more importantly, to pass on his genes, he has to find a female anglerfish as quickly as possible. Once he has found her, he has no time to waste in preliminary courtship rituals. He bites her, releasing an enzyme that bonds their flesh together. Gradually, they become one. He releases his milt (fish sperm) and she fertilises her eggs. Before long, baby anglerfish start the whole lazy cycle again. The female ends up with her late mate's testes dangling out of her side.

The **cod** family belongs to a classification of fish called Gadidae. There are two important species: the North Atlantic cod that can live to the age of 25 and the smaller Pacific cod that attains his majority at 18 but never gets any further than that. When spawning time comes (March and April are key months), the cod congregate in specific areas and dive to a depth of 660ft (200 metres). Among many spawning grounds worldwide, there is one just north of Newquay at the mouth of the Bristol Channel and another near Stornaway.

The mating ritual involves a great deal of muscle-flexing by the macho males who grunt and flap their dorsal and anal fins. When the testosterone level rises, it seems to be a common characteristic of animals – whether they are birds, fish, mammals and most insects – for the males to preen and try to convince the females that they are bigger, stronger and lovelier than they really are.

Once a cod has caught the attention of a female, he will turn upside down and swim beneath her. Coupled like this, they swim in circles while spawning. A female cod lays six million eggs at a time and it takes three weeks for her brood to hatch. The larvae remain in a planktonic stage (very small, drifting organisms) until 10 weeks later when they sink to the seabed and begin feeding on tiny crustaceans amongst the *epifauna*. Within a few weeks they have developed into tiny cod.

The river **crayfish** has to fight to sow his oats. The female crayfish submits only after she has been knocked about a lot. Crayfish are really timid creatures even though they have 12 appendages called *pleopods*, which is the posh name given to their many limbs. They wear suits of armour and prefer moving about at night.

The male crayfish uses his first two pairs of swimming limbs to transfer his little ball of sperm to the lady crayfish's sac situated below her thorax. She starts ovulating by curling up her tail and exerting pressure to release her eggs into the sperm. She inspects and cleans each individual egg she lays – there can be as many as 400 – and then she holds them securely to her abdomen until they hatch about four weeks later, usually in the spring. Mother and children communicate by means of pheromones. Freshwater crayfish eggs are larger than the seawater variety, and they cling to their mother for a considerable period before swimming free.

**Squid** and **cuttlefish** have ten arms. They also possess an enormous number of *chromatophores* (cells containing pigments) that they can use to spontaneously change colour and size. They use this ability mostly in self-defence, although they have more dastardly tricks hidden up their numerous sleeves.

The alpha male of a group of cuttlefish has a harem of females over whom he is fiercely possessive. Because males outnumber females by a ratio of 10:1, the boys without a harem have been known to resort to subterfuge during the mating season. Proportionate to their size, cuttlefish are very brainy.

One trick of the frustrated, young cuttlefish is to disguise himself as a female. This way he can sidle past the boss, sneak into the harem and pretend to be a new concubine. Once inside, the newcomer quickly sheds his false colours and gets down to cuttlefish business.

The actual coupling proceeds with a complex courting display. The male will become rigid and limp by turns. He flourishes his arms in a hypnotic rainbow of changing colours until one of the ladies is overcome by curiosity.

Squid come together in a rippling movement and hold on to each other. On a couple of his arms he has tiny hooks that dig into her to give him stability for the forthcoming act of consummation.

One of the male's arms is larger than the others. This is his special sperm-delivering arm called the *hectocotylus*. While they are in their sexual embrace, this arm takes his spermatophores

– his little sacs of sperm – and carefully deposits them into her spermatheca cavity where her eggs are stored, and sometimes into a cavity in her mouth (called a buccal) where the sperm can be ingested. The toe-curling peculiarity about the male's hectocotylus is that it can sometimes break off inside the female.

Following fertilisation, the female wastes no time in discharging her eggs, which float about in the water in their thousands, while their mother does her best to hide them in safe crevices and holes in the reefs. It takes four to six weeks before the eggs hatch and miniature squid emerge.

The firefly squid is so called because this little fellow, only three inches long, glows like a firefly. He uses this built-in bioluminescence to lure prey to warn off predators or to woo a member of the opposite sex. He lives deep in the Pacific Ocean and his lifespan is just 12 months.

Firefly squid migrate to the shore of Toyama Bay in Japan to lay up to a billion eggs amongst the plankton in shallow waters. Once the eggs have been laid, the life's purpose of mature firefly squid is over and they begin to die. Two weeks later, the firefly squid eggs hatch and the orphans are born into a dangerous environment. Most of them are eaten before they have a chance to take in their surroundings.

**Gobies**: there are more than 2000 species of this little fish, which seldom grows longer than 4ins (10cm) in length. Depending on the species, they can lay from five to 5000 eggs, which are attached to a stony surface such as coral. The male fertilises the eggs and remains on guard until they hatch into larvae a few days later.

Some species, such as the blue-banded goby and the blackeye

goby, can change their sex. They live in colonies dominated by an alpha male and a retinue of females. Should the male get eaten (usually by a cod or a haddock) the female head of the pecking order takes charge. Over a few weeks, her body, including genitals and brain chemistry, changes into a male. If another male arrives in the colony and becomes dominant, the temporary sex-change male will revert back into a female again.

It is desirable for females to display red underbellies if they want to attract males to fertilise their eggs. The girls with plain grey gills tend to find themselves left on the shelf.

**Guppies** (also known as millionfish) are the most popular fish to be kept in home aquariums. Originally, they came from South America. They can perform the most spectacular jumps out of the water reaching speeds of 4ft per second.

When it comes to reproduction, they are fussy about the heat of the water, reluctant to do anything except swim unless the temperature is within a whisker of 26C (69-80F).

The male has a special anal fin called a gonopodium that is tucked behind his ventral fin, and this has evolved into a sort of torpedo tube. When the warmth of the water is just right, he will thrust his gonopodium into the female and fire his missiles into her receptive chamber. His two torpedoes are compact balls of spermatozoa.

The lady guppy has an area near her anus called the gravid spot. Once insemination has taken place, the gravid spot changes colour and becomes dark. After three to four weeks, she will give birth to as many as 30 small-fry. The birthing process takes an hour or two. However, since she is capable of storing sperm for at least a year, she can start the gestation period again whenever she sees fit without the need for a male.

Experiments have taken place to cross-breed guppies with other species, but the resultant hybrids always turn out to be male.

**Herring** belong to the family Clupeidae, which is estimated to include at least 200 species. They are sleek, silver-coloured fish with small heads, found in abundance in the oceans of the Northern hemisphere. They possess single dorsal fins that do not contain spines like other fish and their life expectancy is about 15 years. They travel in huge schools and generally spawn together between late summer and the beginning of winter, producing 50,000 eggs per lay, which are deposited on rocks and seaweed. Male herring will scatter their milt (fish semen) over the area and the eggs hatch after two weeks. They reach sexual maturity at the age of 5.

Fishermen call **mackerel** 'the hardhead'. Spawning occurs from March to October and each female produces up to 400,000 eggs at this time. The survival rate is poor.

**Mosquitofish** are freshwater fish sometimes referred to as *gambusia* – their generic name. A large part of their diet consists of mosquito larvae. At first, this was thought to be a good thing. In the crusade to destroy mosquitoes mosquitofish have been artificially introduced into ecosystems all over the world. What could not be foreseen was that, due to the fiercely aggressive nature of mosquitofish, they fight and kill all sorts of other aquatic creatures that get in their way – frogs, dragonflies and other fish. It is now considered a moot point whether they are more destructive of their habitat than beneficial to it.

To mate, the male mosquitofish opens the rays of a female's gonopodium (a modified anal fin) and inserts milt into her ovary (she has no uterus). She can store his sperm inside her until the temperature is right to spawn. However, the male doesn't always get further than touching her gonopodium. More often than not, the female will reject the male's advances. In laboratory experiments, it has been demonstrated that the female mosquitofish prefer those males who have large sex organs. About three weeks later she will give birth to about 60 small-fry. She is capable of having up to six broods in one season.

There are over 200 species of **pipefish**, and most of them live in seawater. These creatures are related to seahorses but without the noble heads and the floppy mane. Their tails are thin and snake-like. Their courting display is elaborate and it is the lady who initiatives love-play. She will sometimes take two lovers in succession. When pipefish mate, the female ejaculates her eggs onto the male. His body partly absorbs them and he fertilises the embryos. Eventually, the small-fry hatch, detach themselves from their father's body and immediately begin swimming and feeding independently.

**Sticklebacks** used to be called tittlebats. In Britain there are two species of stickleback – the ten-spined and the three-spined. The latter is the more familiar of the two. When the breeding season begins, male sticklebacks' eyes turn a beguiling blue and their bellies change from silver to bright red. They swim into shallower waters and set about building homes for their future families. They burrow into the seabed and line the pit with shells and seaweed, which they bond together with a sort of glue called spiggin – a product exuded from their renal glands. The males change colour, their skins turning bluish – a sign to the females that love is in the air.

To attract the ladies, mature sticklebacks are strongly competitive. The more resourceful males will add shiny objects such as pretty stones and bits of old tin to their bowers, which the females cruise around to inspect until she settles on the one she considers the one most full of bling.

The males entice the females towards their new burrows by performing an underwater dance. They turn this way and that, nudging females closer to the nests.

If she seems amenable, the male will swim on his side and point with his snout towards the centre of the nest. When they are both ensconced, fertilisation takes place. Once the hatchlings appear, the father takes as much pride in nurturing them and keeping them safe as the mother. Often, the mother goes away, leaving the father to take sole charge. He sometimes takes advantage of his mate's absence to entice another female into his burrow and fertilise a second set of eggs. He fans the eggs with his pectoral fin ensuring a steady flow of oxygenated water, continuing to do so until they hatch seven or eight days later.

Some adolescent male sticklebacks who have yet to learn how to build love nests for themselves will pretend to be female sticklebacks and flaunt themselves for love and attention in front of more mature male sticklebacks. When the homosexual interlopers are discovered, the mature males tend to get extremely angry.

**Stingrays** are related to sharks. They have one or more venomous barbed stingers hidden in their tail. The stinger breaks off when the ray hits its target, and the infection of the barb in the wound can cause pain for many years. Two types of ray fish, the porcupine and the manta, do not have stingers.

Stingrays are non-bony fishes and exhibit precise sexual dimorphism – a clear difference between male and female. You can identify a mature male by the two 'claspers' on either side of his tail. A courting male will shadow the female of choice before biting at her pectoral disc. Then he places one of his claspers into her vulva area and the rest is sheer fertilisation – the reason that W C Fields gave for his aversion to imbibing water.

Gestation lasts three months. The embryos are held in suspension in the mother's womb which has no placenta. Embryos receive their nutrition from a yolk sac and just before birth the mother provides milk in her uterus. She gives birth to live litters of six to 12. The youngsters are functionally developed and identical in all but size to their parents. A female stingray is capable of storing semen in her body in order to delay parturition until she feels the timing is right.

A few **sturgeon** live in freshwater lakes, but most of them spend their lives at sea and only migrate to fresh water to breed. Slow as they are to put on weight, they can eventually grow to 12ft in length. They are harvested for their roe – caviar – depleting their ability to breed. Left alone, a sturgeon can lay 6,000,000 offspring every year for 35 years. They are coveted by the rich who consider caviar a delicacy with the result that sturgeon are on the verge of extinction. The maximum recorded life span of a lake sturgeon is 152 years.

# FLEAS

*Locusts in trees do it, bees do it,*
*Even over-educated fleas do it...*
(LYRICS BY COLE PORTER)

Fleas are wingless insects whose diet consists exclusively of blood, thus their major occupation is finding a suitable host. Cats, dogs, humans, cattle – any animal containing blood is the equivalent of Fortnum and Masons to a flea.

Thanks to their exceptionally long hind legs they can leap as high as 7ins (18cm), and they can do the long-jump straight forwards to a distance of 13ins (33cm).

When a male and a female flea encounter each other in the hairy jungle, they indulge in foreplay by each sucking a drop of blood to give them sustenance to mate. Proportional to its size, the male flea has the biggest and most complicated penis of any insect. It has hooks and spikes and knobbly bits. The act of copulation lasts for hours as it is difficult for the male to disengage.

A female flea drinks blood at the rate of 15 times her own body weight daily. Within 48 hours of mating, she starts laying eggs and is capable of laying up to 50 every day – 4000 eggs in her lifetime. Given the right humidity, the eggs will hatch within a week. The larvae are like tiny caterpillars. At first, they eat the faeces of their parents. This practice – called coprophagy – is more common in creatures than might be supposed. For example, it's a gourmet's delight for rabbits. The faeces contain immunising properties that are passed on to the offspring.

All fleas prefer darkness to light. The larvae spin themselves into a tiny silken cocoon that shields them from light and helps to disguise their presence. Eventually, when the heat is right, adult fleas will emerge and within 10 seconds start digging around for blood. The flea has two parts to its mouth. One part pierces the skin of the host and inserts saliva while the other part sucks out blood. Mating is the next thing on the agenda and the lifecycle of the flea starts all over again.

There is a type of flea that lives exclusively on rabbits. This flea can detect from the antibodies in the rabbit's blood when the rabbit is about to give birth. The flea then times the birth of her own eggs accordingly and as soon as they hatch, the caterpillar fleas move down onto the newly born rabbits where they start their life cycle all over again.

## FLEHMEN RESPONSE

A number of mammals, including ungulates and felids, possess a *vomeronasal* organ situated in the roof of their mouths behind their front teeth. This is an extra-sensitive taste bud that can detect the hormonal condition of the other animals by responding to the pheromones given off by them, known as the 'flehmen response' (a phrase you will encounter several times in this book). Similarly, when you see a horse with its head held high and displaying its gnashers, the most likely reason for such behaviour is to 'test the air' (known as a gustatory investigation).

As well as judging whether another animal is likely to be sexually receptive, the flehmen response can convey to a male animal which of several offspring belong to his gene pool and whether or not a female has just given birth.

## FLIES (*SEE ALSO INSECTS*)

*The dragonflies, in the reeds, do it.*
*Sentimental centipedes do it...*
(LYRICS BY COLE PORTER)

There are 80,000 species of fly (*muscidae*), the most common being Musca Domestica – the common housefly. To reproduce, the male hops on to the female, rubs his front legs against his beloved's head, after which she quickly succumbs. The life cycle of a fly is eight weeks: first they are eggs, then maggots, and finally back to flies.

The hoverfly has the longest tongue tube in the animal kingdom. It feeds on the iris amongst other deep-welled flowers. The eye of a housefly detects motion. It does not 'see things' as humans do. Therefore, it is possible to kill a housefly by approaching it very, very slowly. Flies don't like flying in the dark.

**Botflies**: the lady botfly's anatomy includes a pouch-like appendage called an oviduct in which she hatches her eggs until they become baby botflies, or as we generally call them, maggots.

The caring mother will then look for a host body to act as a maggot nursery. She looks for something not too warm and not too moist but just right. Generally she finds the perfect crèche in the noses of sheep. Here the maggots chew away through the membranes and into the nice juicy sinuses. From there it is but a short tunnel to reach the brain. The unwitting host – the sheep – tends to stagger at this stage and unless put out of its misery by a kindly shepherd it will die an agonising death.

The sexual technique of the **dragonfly** requires a gift for gymnastics. The male grasps his partner by her neck with his feet. Once he has got the hang of this, he clings onto her by the hooks on his tail while they are still airborne. Then he persistently bangs her head against his genitals.

A female dragonfly – *Calopteryx Virgo* ('the maiden with beautiful wings') – can see round her own body at an angle of 360 degrees. Each eye contains 28,000 lenses. After two years lying around as an ugly grub, it metamorphoses into a beautiful creature for only 12 days. The male immediately sets out his territory – 12ft square – where he conducts all marital matters. First, he has to produce a tankful of sperm, which he does in a masturbatory manner, to fill up his front sex organ. When a female prances into his territory, he grabs her by the throat with his legs. They fly around exciting each other until she places her aperture against his sperm sac. In a state of ecstasy, they fly in circles (described as 'a mating wheel'). When he has released his sperm, he takes her down to his own cherished territory next to water where he helps her to lay down her eggs just under the surface of a specially chosen plant.

The male dragonfly is cavalier when courting and aggressively protects his mate and the site on which they have chosen to lay their eggs and rear their family. Some have been known to dive-bomb humans who have ventured too close.

The **firefly** attracts its mate by lighting up. Hundreds of thousands of these fellows sit in trees flashing away like Piccadilly Circus. Their luminescence can be seen from miles away. Guided by the lights, frustrated lady fireflies make a beeline (or should that be called a 'firefly line'?) for the lights. Eager for love, the ladies are not satisfied until they've put the lights out.

There's a compartment in the abdomen of a firefly that contains a sac of nitric oxide. In the mating season, chemical reactions trigger off the gas to produce quite a bright glow. The flashes of light that come from within the firefly's stomach act as a beacon to female fireflies whose own nitric oxide processes respond. As they seek each other out and get closer to each other, they look like a bunch of fairy lights.

The male **fruitfly** starts his courtship by tasting the object of his fancy with the tips of his feet. If she doesn't kick him away, he goes on to rub his feet on her vagina – evidently a turn-on for the female fruitfly who initiates a brief but intense few seconds of consummation. The female fruitfly lays about 100 eggs at a time. Over the spawning season she can produce 2000 eggs.

The **greenfly** propagates without benefit of male intervention. She produces fertile eggs from her ovum, and many a grumpy gardener will complain at the overnight garland of voracious greenfly larvae sticking to flowers and fruit bushes and sucking them dry. All the little greenflies are female and within a short time the next generation exude a covering of eggs over the same angry gardener's favourite plants.

The **mayfly** takes several years to develop from a water grub into its beauteous adult state. And then the male has just 24 hours in which to get a sex-life. To draw attention to himself, he hovers about 18ins into the air before fluttering down again.

Rhythmically, he repeats this dance for a couple of hours until dusk, by which time, with luck, a lady mayfly's curiosity is aroused sufficiently for her to fly over and join in. Together they rise and fall in a ballet of joyful copulation. Thousands of mayflies cuddle together and dance in shimmering unison. As the sun sets, the females expel their eggs into the water where the offspring spend several years as water grubs, most of them ending up as frog food.

## FOXES

The gestation period for foxes is between 51 and 63 days. They are part of the dog family. They live in family groups but always hunt alone. For mating habits, see the section on dogs.

## FROGS AND TOADS

Frogs, like crocodiles, waste no time in foreplay. The croaking of the frog is a mating call. If no lady frog responds, the croaking can go on for days, or until his voice gives out or, in extremis, he dies of frustration.

The male frog clings onto the back of a female for as long as it takes for her to lay some eggs that he can immediately inseminate. This lengthy balancing act in the mounted position is known as amplexus.

Some frogs spawn more eggs than they can possibly handle so that they can be used as a food source if the outlook is bleak.

The Vaquero frog makes sure of fertilisation by mating with several horny female frogs before they lay their eggs. Inside the male frogs a special accouchement sac develops, so when the males, subsequent to fertilisation, swallow the eggs they are, in fact, actually protecting them. Parturition takes place when the males regurgitate the tadpoles.

Tree frogs of South America have red eyes, three eyelids and long, strong limbs and fingers to enable them to climb. Despite their vivid colours, they are not venomous. The bright colours are part of their defence system. When threatened, they display their sticky, orange feet, puff out their yellow and blue-green bodies whilst simultaneously opening their blood-red eyes as wide as possible. Such behaviour has a name – 'startle colouration'. This astonishing sight, together with the intense display, mesmerises potential predators long enough for the frogs to escape. These tiny red-eyed tree frogs wait for the rainy season before mating, which usually occurs between March and October. There is often rivalry between males for a female and the males try to knock each other off the branches. Such struggles can happen just as a male is about to mount the female, causing a mountain of frogs to pile on top of her.

The tiny arrow poison frogs (also known as poison dart frogs – in particular, the species of *Phyllobates terribilis*) of South America are so venomous that, according to David Attenborough, 'one ten-thousandth of a gram of their poison is enough to kill a man'. Indians living in the forests use their poison to smear the darts used in blow-pipes. These frogs are brightly coloured, basically as a warning signal that they are poisonous. Potential predators have learned to keep their distance. Another advantage of being vividly coloured, at least from the male's point of view, is that a female, when selecting a mate, always opts for the male with the brightest display of colours.

However, these little poisonous frogs are dedicated parents, carrying the newly hatched tadpoles on their backs and into the safety of their nests or 'canopies' as they are more accurately described. In the manner of fish, the female poison frog lays a cluster of eggs, which is then fertilised by the male. They are fiercely territorial, and fights break out between them for possession of the best nests, quite often eating each others' eggs.

Medical science is developing pain-killing drugs from some of these poisonous frogs. Epibatidine is one chemical extract alleged to be 200 times as potent as morphine.

# G

## GEESE

In the Greylag Goose community there is a tendency towards homosexuality. Boys will be boys, as they say; and the girls – miffed at losing out – eagerly insinuate themselves between the two males, often getting themselves pregnant in the process.

Geese and swans mate for life – astonishingly staying together for 50 years or longer. A widowed goose or a drake widower sinks into a deep depression, continually searching for the lost partner.

Widow ganders have been known to set up shop together in a largely platonic relationship. Sometimes another lonely goose will come along and fall in love with one of the odd couple. This can result in a *ménage a trois*.

## GIRAFFES

*I'm sure giraffes, on the sly, do it,*
*Heavy hippopotami do it...*
(LYRICS BY COLE PORTER)

The neck of a giraffe certainly helps him to reach leaves high on trees but it makes mating hard work. The female giraffe goes into oestrus fairly frequently – every two or three weeks – and when this happen she swings her hips and swishes her tail in a saucy manner. The male giraffe is not devoid of natural urges, but the effort it takes to mount a female is so great that the male summons up the energy only when he believes there is a good chance she will get pregnant. On the occasions when a male happens upon a frisky female, he will first perform the flehmen response to see if she is in oestrus. First, he nudges her rump to induce urination. He tastes it and if the vintage is to his liking, he begins to court her.

Actually, when a giraffe goes courting, it's quite basic. The male follows her around until she gives in and lets him have his way. However, female giraffes have been known to be a tease. Just as the male thinks he is about to have a jolly afternoon, the female can easily become distracted by another mature male giraffe passing by, particularly if he happens to be sporting more ripply muscles. This waywardness has given female giraffes a reputation for being fickle. The sexual act is disappointingly short for a giraffe. Typically, it lasts less than a minute. The male gets his own back by ignoring her if she becomes pregnant.

The gestation period is usually 457 days. The mother gives

birth from a standing position to one calf only. At the moment of birth, the baby falls to the ground and it takes a little while to recover and struggle to its feet but within an hour, the calf is usually walking around pestering its mother for milk.

As well as long necks, they have long tongues – over a foot long – enabling them to reach the uppermost and most succulent leaves. The strain of pumping blood along that long slender neck and down those long thin legs necessitates a strong heart muscle. The heart walls of giraffes are 3ins thick. Their eyesight is incredible – they can see with focused accuracy up to three miles away. Other animals are aware of this and sometimes trail a herd of giraffe for protection, knowing that at the first sign of danger, however far off it may be, they will be given a head start for a quick getaway.

## GOATS

A virgin goat doe can reach sexual maturity at the age of six months after which she comes into a state of oestrus every three weeks or so on several occasions in the autumn as the weather gets cooler. The period she remains in heat can vary from a few hours to a couple of days, so the timing of consummation is fairly critical.

The doe rarely needs much time before submitting to a buck's advances. Once she takes an interest, she rapidly wags her tail (called 'flagging') and leaks a little urine. The pheromones from this evoke the flehmen response from alert bucks who react by urinating over themselves and rubbing their noses in it.

Mature bucks are constantly at war with each other – fighting for food, drink, shelter or sex. When a doe comes into heat, the bucks fight each other to establish a pecking order. Junior bucks, finding themselves in the middle of a herd for the first time, narrowly avoid buggery from the older, more excitable males.

When the winning buck has established mating supremacy, the doe acknowledges his presence by squatting and emitting a stream of urine. The buck puts his nose into this stream and, satisfied that she is not teasing him, canters alongside her as she literally leads him on a chase to a place of her choosing where she will submit. During this token show of feminine modesty, the buck makes loud clucking noises in a boisterous and excited way. The gestation period for goats is between 136 to 160 days.

The winning buck can breed with 40 does in a couple of breeding cycles. It is not for nothing that an elderly human roué often acquires the reputation of being 'an old goat'.

## GONOPODS

Some creatures use a 'gonopod' instead of a penis. A spider's gonopod is called a maxillary palp. A squid's gonopod is called a hectocotylus. Male millipedes have genital appendage gonopods, by which they transfer the sperm sacs to the female's genital opening.

## GRASSHOPPERS AND CRICKETS

The male grasshopper's mating chirrup has been measured at between 6 and 10 kilohertz. According to the paper 'Functional Ecology', in urban areas nowadays, because of the build-up of traffic noise – measured at between 5 and 7 kilohertz – the roadside grasshoppers have had to chirrup louder and now their peak has shifted towards 10 kilohertz.

The grasshopper, when randy, will rub various bits of itself – legs and wing – together, which produces an annoying chirruping sound. The female of the species finds this a fascinating and flattering turn-on. She follows the chirrups and stands nearby, putting on a seductive pose. Well, it's the same old story. One thing leads to another. There is a lot of pillow talk before they each decide there's a whole world out there waiting to be explored and they go off on their individual and solitary ways.

Of incidental interest (although fascinating for a female **katydid**) the male katydid possesses the largest pair of testes proportionate to its body size of any animal. By the way, katydids are members of the grasshopper family. They leap vast distances and flutter their wings, though they do not fly. They are green and are very good at disguising themselves as leaves.

They sing only at night and each species has its own song, but the words are the same: 'katydid, katy-didn't' over and over again. Apparently, this monotonous sound is produced by rubbing the left forewing against a ridge on the right one.

## GUINEA PIGS

*Old sloths who hang down from twigs do it,*
*Though the effort is great,*
*Sweet guinea pigs do it,*
*Buy a couple and wait...*
(LYRICS BY COLE PORTER)

The male guinea pig waggles his hips in a provocative way in front of the female before chasing her with a view to mate. With luck, she will allow him to mount her and continue waggling his hips. If this is sufficiently pleasing to the female, she relaxes enough to allow copulation to take place. The gestation period for guinea pigs is between 58 and 75 days.

## GULLS

There are 56 species of gull including the kittiwakes. The old name for them was 'mew'. They are intelligent birds with a complex method of communication and a highly developed social structure. They mate for life but divorce is not unknown. Like albatrosses they return to the area of their old nesting sites every year.

In common with most birds, during the breeding season, the gulls' cloacae swell and protrude slightly. The males produce sperm that is stored in their cloacae until the opportunity arises for them to transfer it into the females' cloacae from whence it travels to fertilise their ova.

Gulls, like pigeons, bill and coo, with the males showing off their health and prowess to influence the females' choice, although more often than not, the same breeding pairs come back together year after year.

Once the actual mating takes place, the male climbs onto the back of the female who hunches herself to give her mate a better balancing position. She shifts her tail to one side exposing her cloaca. He arches his body until his cloaca makes a connection with hers. The transfer of sperm takes a matter of seconds. The 'cloacal kiss' is complete.

The size of gull colonies varies from a few pairs to over a hundred thousand pairs. Within these colonies the mating pairs are defensively territorial. Mating couples bond with building nests, which are usually built on the ground. Some species, such as the kittiwakes nest on cliffs. Others, such as Bonaparte's gulls nest in trees.

Typical clutch size is three eggs. Curiously, within a large colony, the females somehow synchronise the timing of laying. Male and female share incubation duties that last from three to four weeks. Once the eggs have hatched, it takes another two weeks of brooding before the chicks are fully fledged.

# H

## HAMSTERS AND GERBILS

Cuddly as they seem, golden hamsters (also known as Syrian hamsters) are rodents and their preference is to live the solitary life. To avoid predators, they remain underground in daylight, which is one of the reasons they prefer to mate at night. Over the years, this has resulted in their being colour blind and having poor vision. An acute sense of smell compensates, and the use of musky scents and pheromones suffices for them to keep track of each other. Female hamsters' reproductive lives are short – no more than a year and a half – but they can give birth to a litter of up to 18 pups at a time. They breed between April and October. When a female is in oestrus she gives off a musky smell and squeaks excitedly, sometimes in the ultrasonic range. The gestation period for hamsters is between 15 to 17 days. They are weaned within three weeks.

Unlike hamsters, gerbils in the wild live in hierarchic groups, with a dominant male and his mate at the top of the pyramid, who are the chief progenitors of pups for the clan. Gerbils mate for life and are faithful till death do them part. In the interim they mate a lot. If the female has given birth in the morning, she might remain disinclined to engage in carnal relations again until the evening.

When the female is in the mood she flounces in front of the male until he follows her and starts thumping his feet – a sign that he is getting keen on the idea. She bows down and he mounts her. The result will be known a mere three weeks later.

## HEDGEHOGS

In Britain over the last 60 years, hedgehog numbers have declined from 30,000,000 to 1,000,000. Hedgehogs have the ability to roll themselves into tiny balls of prickles but on the highways, this is no defence. Tens of thousands of hedgehogs are killed on the roads of Britain every year.

They reach sexual maturity at the age of two. They come out of winter hibernation, put on weight and are ready for a little consummation on a warm night at the beginning of May.

Mating is accompanied by a lot of squealing and chasing. The boar chases the sow who with suitable modesty reacts coyly. They spit at each other and butt heads together and after this strange courtship is over, the lady lowers her quills, spreads herself on the ground and raises her bottom into the air. The actual act of intercourse is all over within two minutes. The boar treks off on another foraging expedition and, with luck, the sow will have her litter about four weeks later.

The sow prepares a burrow for her new family, nicely lined with grass and leaves. The hoglets are born with short white hair that in time grow into spines. It takes a further four weeks for the babies to be weaned. They hang around with mother for another eight weeks by which time they are old enough to go off and fend for themselves. If only they weren't such road hogs.

## HIPPOPOTAMUSES

*Heavy hippopotami do it*
(LYRIC BY COLE PORTER)

Hippopotamus is from the Greek meaning 'horse of the river', and that says it all really. Hippos have hardly any hair, are shaped like enormous barrels, are semi-aquatic and have no territorial claims at all. They are cousins to the whale. To look at one, you might be fooled into thinking they are sweet, fat, loveable creatures. In fact, they are one of the most aggressive animals in the world.

Hippos possess a small tail that they can rotate at high speed. They are known to employ this trick, spinning their tails like propellers, whilst at the same time urinating and defecating. This is designed to spread their faeces over as wide an area as possible and mark out their tiny territory. A lady hippo finds the allure of the resulting scent irresistible.

The pair go into the water to mate and somewhere between 220 and 255 days later, the female will give birth in the water. The calves have to swim to the surface before taking their first breath, after which they become breathers of air.

Females reach sexual maturity at the age of 6 and remain

sexually active all year round. Males are typically a year older before they are ready to mate. Conception takes place at the end of the wet season in summer. After becoming pregnant, a female hippo does not ovulate again for about a year and a half. If the calves find that they are out of their depth in the water, they climb onto their mother's back and she escorts them to safety. It takes a year before a baby hippo is fully weaned. They only venture out of water at night to eat.

## HORSES

When a stallion curls back his upper lip and bares his teeth, it's a sign that there is some odour in the air that he wants to pin down. In the mating season, he tries to detect the pheromones given off in a mare's urine. This is all part of the flehmen response, common to many mammals. Sometimes, the reason for a horse bearing his teeth with a sort of snarl is simply so he can acquaint himself with a strange visitor. Very rarely is it due to something having tickled his sense of humour. The gestation period for horses is between 329 to 345 days.

## HUMANS

*The Dutch in old Amsterdam do it,*
*Not to mention the Finns.*
*Folks in Siam do it,*
*think of Siamese twins...*
(LYRICS BY COLE PORTER)

The human female is the only mammal not to be constrained

in sexual pleasure by the period of oestrus. Humans indulge in monogamy, polygamy and polyandry. There seems there is nothing that a human will not try if he or she thinks it will give pleasure. It is calculated that if, in the last 2000 years, humans had been subject to the same evolutionary restraints as other animals there would be barely a million human beings alive today.

However, Sir David Attenborough, in his book *The Trials of Life* states: '...For the vast majority of higher animals, sexuality with all its hazards and complications is the only route to reproduction...'

The flushed pink of genital labia indicates a state of arousal. Our close cousins, the chimps and bonobos would recognise this at once and waste no time in taking advantage of the knowledge. Humans are subtler.

Pheromones are so subtle that humans cannot necessarily detect them, but smell is important. In French, a woman's personal aroma is called her *'cassolette'*. A man's sense of smell is not as acute as that of a woman. She sprays synthetic pheromones in the form of perfume, and lipstick is used instinctively by a woman of the world to complement the colour of her vulva. Men take an interest without necessarily realising what is causing their curiosity. An astute man takes care to make himself olefactorily fresh by the use of deodorants and aftershaves. This has a pleasurable effect upon his female counterpart who has been known to sleep with her partner's pyjamas on the pillow when he is absent.

As ovulation approaches, the human female tends to take a more provocative approach to her style of dressing. At the same time, her voice becomes higher pitched.

The London School of Economics has made a study about the

best time to have sex. It reveals that 'natural cortisol levels, which stimulate sex hormones, are at their peak on Thursday mornings'.

The average life expectancy for a man in the UK is 78.1years. The average life expectancy for a woman in the UK is 82.1 years. The gestation period for humans is between 253 to 303 days.

The average spermatozoa count of a 35-year-old French male in 1989 was 73.8 per millilitre. By 2005, this had dropped to 49.9 per millilitre. (From the journal, *Human Reproduction*). We are not told if it was the same Frenchman.

Luteinizing hormone is a key building block of female sexual desire and is one of the triggers that gears up the female sex-drive.

In mammals, which of the partners determines the chromosomes of the offspring's sex? In 335 BC, Aristotle postulated that if the heat of a male overwhelmed that of the female during copulation, then a male baby would develop – and vice versa. This belief persisted until about 100 years ago.

Something like this is true of reptiles but in humans, sex is determined chromosomally. The norm is for the male cells to contain an X and a Y chromosome whereas female cells contain two X chromosomes. It's the presence or absence of the Y chromosome that determines the sex of the offspring.

The American Psychiatric Association retained homosexuality as a mental disease until 1973.

The average length of an adult male human's penis is five inches. The human clitoris is just the tip of the iceberg. There is much more going on below the surface where it is connected to two bulbs situated either side of the vaginal cavity. Dr Ernst Grafenberg discovered a small area hidden by the clitoris that he claimed was the central part of orgasmic activity in women. This piece of anatomy, hidden above the vaginal wall surrounding the urethra, has come to be called the 'G spot' named after Doctor Grafenberg. Apparently, it can be difficult to find but it often pays dividends to spend a few happy hours in an exploratory hunt for it. The longer the search the more lubricated the state of a woman's mucosal tissue. Who doesn't enjoy a treasure hunt?

In 1948, at Indiana University, Alfred C Kinsey produced an unexpected bestseller called *Sexual Behaviour in the Human Male*, followed in 1953 by *Sexual Behaviour in the Human Female* (written with W B Pomeroy and C E Martin). The revelatory results of the surveys revealed that 92 per cent of men masturbate, that 70 per cent of couples indulge in oral sex, that practically everyone has premarital sex and about half of married couples have at least one extracurricular affair.

Critics have raised concerns about the way data was collected for the Kinsey report. They maintain that volunteers for the study must have included a disproportionate number of sexual deviants.

Two decades later William H Masters and Virginia E Johnson published two new studies: *Human Sexual Response* (1968) and *Human Sexual Inadequacy* (1970). These books postulated that vaginal and clitoral orgasmic responses were identical.

The chief findings from this study led to what has become known as 'the human sexual response cycle', as follows:

1) The initial arousal or 'excitement phase'
2) The full arousal prior to orgasm stage 'the plateau'
3) Orgasm
4) Post orgasm – 'the resolution phase'

They confirmed that for men there is a 'refractory period' after orgasm during which they cannot ejaculate again. A woman has no refractory period and can orgasm any number of times. It is difficult to believe that it took scientists so many years to reach these conclusions.

They came to another disputed conclusion: that during copulation, 70 per cent of women achieved enough clitoral stimulation through thrusting alone for a woman to achieve orgasm.

It also volunteered the following information: 'In answer to the question, "Have you had a homosexual experience?" 22 per cent of 1335 men said "yes" and 17 per cent of 1384 women said "yes". What it does not say is who was telling the truth.

According to the Kinsey Report (in 1948) the frequency of the sexual act within marriage is 2.8 times per week in the late teens. By the age of 30 this is reduced to 2.2 times per week. When you've reached 50 you're lucky to get it once a week. During the sex act, on average 70 per cent of mean reach orgasm but only 30 per cent of women achieve the same conclusion.

## HUMMINGBIRDS

These are very tiny birds. One species – the Bee Hummingbird – is only 5cm long. They can go into a state of self-induced hibernation when food is in short supply. They are the only known type of bird that can fly backwards and they get their name because of the humming sound produced by the beating of their wings. They may live for as long as 10 years.

In early spring, when a male hummingbird wants to mate (particularly an *Archilochus colubris*) he puts on a flying display and shows off to the ladies. He does loop-the-loops, figure-eights, and any other flights of fancy he can muster. At the same time, he squawks and sings and tempts a female to join him. Sometimes she succumbs and they can face each other in the air while hovering up and down like a couple of miniature helicopters. They have been known to mate in the air, on the ground and in trees.

For birds, the physical act of mating is a brief affair. They merely have to join their cloacae for a few seconds to transfer semen from him into her. Then he's on his way to another courting display with a different bird. The female builds a nest for her forthcoming egg-laying event – generally two eggs, which she sits on for two weeks until they hatch.

## HYENAS

As well as being aggressively bossy, the female hyena is bigger and stronger than her male counterpart and is easily mistaken for a male hyena because her anatomy includes a pseudopenis, which is, in fact, an enlarged clitoris that she can cause to erect at will.

In order to mate, the gentler sex – that is to say, the male in the case of hyenas – has to insert his penis into her pseudopenis. This is as difficult as threading cotton through the eye of a needle. However, the existence of a thriving population of hyenas testifies to the fact that it can be done.

Eventually, the female has to give birth through the same pseudopenis, and one imagines this is not something for the squeamish to witness. And with females having to endure such a difficult birthing procedure, it is perhaps not entirely surprising that a clan of hyenas is ruled with a rod of iron by a matriarchal female.

Biologist Laurence Frank has described other odd behaviour

peculiar to hyenas, including the way they say hello to each other. After being separated for a few hours, spotted hyenas engage in 'greeting' displays that entail lifting their legs and exposing their erect genitalia for inspection. Subordinate females often initiate greetings and this is the only known case of an erection being a submissive gesture.

'This unusual display is not without its risks [because] each hyena puts its reproductive organs in immediate proximity to very powerful jaws,' adds Frank. 'On the rare occasions when the aggression escalates to fighting, the resulting damage may be severe enough to destroy or seriously compromise the reproductive competence of the injured party.'

Of all animals, the cubs of a spotted hyena are amongst those few who are pre-disposed to attacking and killing their siblings.

## HYMENOPTERA

The literal meaning of this word is 'membrane-winged', which covers an order of insects including bees, ants and wasps. What they have in common is two pairs of wings. The females have an *ovipositor* that can be adapted for stinging, piercing or sawing.

## IGUANAS

Iguanas are vegetarian lizards that hail from the Americas. They can reach 6ft in length and they have a third eye – the parietal eye – on their foreheads. Nobody is certain of its function except to speculate that it can probably tell day from night and what time of the year it is.

Galapagos land iguanas become sexually mature at some point between the ages of 8 and 15. When a female iguana is in oestrus, the males are extremely aggressive. Mating seasons vary and the eggs hatch from three to four months later. They have been largely wiped out since the introduction of cats, dogs and rats. They share the same plight as the New Zealand kiwi. Frantic efforts are being made to save them.

## INSECTS (*SEE ALSO BUGS*)

The raison d'être of all insects is procreation. They spend most of their lives trying to mate and to this end they employ sophisticated navigational systems. For example, the common housefly has compound eyes and a strong sense of smell. The housefly (*Musca domestica*) comprises about 91 per cent of all flies encountered in human habitation.

When a male fly deploys his senses to detect a potential mate he will grapple with her in mid-air and consummation will take place during flight, mounting her from behind. Copulation rarely takes longer than a few seconds. Soon after fertilisation, the female housefly lays her eggs – any number between 80 and 150. They hatch within a few hours and maggots emerge. Changing into pupae is dependent on the conditions – the temperature and the availability of food (faeces are a popular snack). It can take anything from one day to one week for this transformation to occur.

The female fly is sexually active within 36 hours of emerging from the pupa. The average lifespan of a common housefly is little more than two weeks. The female normally mates only once and from that one encounter she will store enough sperm to enable her to repeatedly lay sets of eggs.

Nearly all insects exude pheromones to attract the opposite sex. Female fireflies use visual signals such as glowing in the dark to show they are available.

## INVERTEBRATES

The word 'invertebrate' refers to any animal species without a backbone, or to be more technical, those animals without a vertebral column. Sponges, worms, snails, starfish are all invertebrates. The fact is, 98 per cent of all animals in the world are invertebrates.

## JELLYFISH AND ANEMONES

Jellyfish are an invertebrate type of animal – they have no bones. There are many kinds of jellyfish, usually delineated according to their body shape. The 'box jellyfish' (in a subclass called Cubozoa), which has 24 eyes, are the easiest to describe.

The bodies of these creatures can grow to 10ft in length and nearly 1ft across. Their bodies are bell-shaped and these types of jellyfish are often referred to as *medusae*. They mate on an annual basis and their courtship ritual is interesting to watch. The male and the female entangle with their tentacles until they get into a position of a close embrace. Their mouths are on the underside of their bodies and the male will appear to kiss the lady but in fact he is presenting her with his sperm packet (a *spermatophore*). This is ingested by the female jellyfish and once inside her, her eggs become fertilised.

For other types of jellyfish there are variations on this theme, but the end result is the same: fry called planulae. In time the planulae develop into polyps and eventually they grow into jellyfish. Some of them have been given the name 'sea wasps' because they have a very painful sting that has been known to kill humans.

The *Turritopsis dohrnii*, otherwise known as 'the immortal medusae', have one of the most curious life cycles: they never die. This life form is a *hydrozoa* – something between a jellyfish and a coral. It lives in warm waters such as the Mediterranean. It has neither heart nor brain. It has one orifice, which acts as both mouth and anus. In the beginning (for want of a better expression) it is a polyp like a coral attached to a firm surface. Then it 'buds' into a medusoid, which swims freely and gradually changes into a medusa that attaches itself to rocks and finally metamorphosises into a polyp. It has turned full circle and the polyp has regenerated itself. Sometimes it will produce two buds and thus the population of the species imperceptibly increases.

The sea wasp jellyfish has the most poisonous sting of any animal in the world. Death from a sting can come within three minutes. And the sea is full of them.

# K

## KANGAROOS AND WALLABIES

*The chimpanzees, in the zoos, do it,*
*Some courageous kangaroos do it...*
(LYRICS BY COLE PORTER)

In the late 18th century, the people who first stumbled across kangaroos borrowed from the aborigine language to give it a name: 'cunquroo' became kangaroo.

Permit me a diversionary, but apposite, anecdote at this point. Many moons ago when I was young man in search of sex and sensuality, I was acting with 'Vivien Leigh and the Old Vic Company' on a world tour. I'm not name-dropping – that's how the tour was billed. Vivien had recently divorced Sir Laurence Olivier, and the purpose of the tour was to remove Vivien from the scene at a sensitive period in English theatrical history while Larry was at the helm of Chichester and the National Theatre. Oh yes – and as a bonus we were to entertain the world with some plays.

After several months in the Antipodes, the company needed time to transport the scenery to America, so the players were given a holiday. I went to the Great Barrier Reef with my friend, Patrick Stewart. (Now I *am* name-dropping.) I mean, of course, *Sir* Patrick Stewart.

We holidayed at Quoin Island, a tropical paradise so named by Captain Cook because it is in the shape of a wedge – that is to say, quoin-shaped. It seemed remote although actually it was not far from the mainland. Anyway, it was barely a mile in length and at its widest point no more than half a mile. Apart from a caretaker who had taken to renting out primitive holiday huts, it was uninhabited save for two troops (or mobs) of kangaroos – each on either end of the island. Baby kangaroos – joeys – were to be seen all over the place and we wiled away many an amusing hour holding out empty sacks for the joeys to jump into. Anything that looked like a pouch was home for them. They felt safe in a sack. That's when I developed a lifelong interest in kangaroos, albeit from a distance.

Kangaroos are in a family of animals known as Macropodidae ('big foot'). In the 18th century, the word was taken from the language of the local people who lived in the area of modern-day Cooktown. Sir Joseph Banks's diary entry for 12 July 1770 records the sighting of a 'kanguru'.

Kangaroos thump the earth with their tails if they sense danger. The pack will scatter leaving behind the dominant male to defend his entourage. There are large kangaroos – the great red can grow to over 7ft tall. There are also tiny kangaroos such as the musky rat-kangaroo – these, it will come as no surprise, are about the size of a rat.

Then there are big-foots that come in all sizes in between. These include the wallabies, the quokkas, the tree kangaroos, the pademelons and the wallaroos. There are also distant cousins such as the potoroos (even smaller than rat-size) and bettongs (barely weighing in at a couple of kilograms each).

The musky rat-kangaroo (the only surviving member of the Hypsiprymnodontidae family) lives in the rainforests of north-east Australia. It is no more than 24cm long and it eats fruit and climbs trees.

Kangaroos are of that order of mammals known as marsupials. They graze in the cool of the night and laze in the heat of the day. They are unusual in several respects. For example, the male's penis grows *below* his testes. The female has three vaginas: one is for giving birth, the second is for sex and the third is a spare for more sex because she has two wombs.

Red kangaroos live in loose mobs of about a dozen animals. When the males are feeling frisky (usually spring, though there is no set breeding season) they begin fighting in order to gain dominance over the females. Their hind legs are powerful weapons, and one flick of their tail can cause serious damage. Whichever buck backs off first is the loser. The fights are highly ritualised.

Once he has established his presence, the buck hops around sniffing a lot and testing the air for a doe in oestrus. When he finds her, he starts scratching the doe's tail. This serves as foreplay. If she reciprocates, the lady will raise her tail. Her mate will sit back on his own tail and put his forepaws round her to hold her in place. He edges forward until his genital area touches her cloaca. The magic is soon over, but the buck doesn't stop here; he goes on to the next doe and smells her urine (the flehmen response) and if she's about ready, he will make overtures.

Following coition, it takes between three and four weeks for an embryonic joey to be born. Just before parturition occurs, the female kangaroo diligently licks the hair on her stomach from the pouch down to her cloaca until a narrow pathway has been formed.

Blind and virtually helpless except for a reflex action in its forepaw muscles and hardly more than an inch in height, the wriggly butterbean struggles upwards along the groove in the stomach fur made by his mother. Edging itself up with its tiny forepaws, this tiny foetus jack-knifes itself through the furrow until it finds the pouch (known as a marsupium) and drops in. This journey normally takes no more than three minutes. There, its little mouth searches until it locates one of her four teats to which it attaches itself for grim life. It will be at least 200 days before it is strong enough and sufficiently confident to leave the pouch.

Whilst continuing to feed her joey, the female kangaroo can get pregnant again but she has the unique ability to retain the fertilised egg in her womb as a *blastocyst*. This embryo will not mature until her current joey leaves the pouch. Simultaneously, she may have three joeys in three separate stages of development: one starting to hop, one in her pouch and one waiting in her womb. Once they start lactating after pregnancy, female kangaroos go on producing different grades of milk for the rest of their lives.

The Western Grey kangaroo differs slightly from the red in terms of mob structure. Here, the mob is dominated by females: the queen doe, her daughters and their joeys. The bucks squabble to get into the right pecking order, but their first fancy is the queen doe followed by the daughters in order of dominance. Joeys generally leave the pouch after around 10 months but they continue to be nursed for an additional eight months.

The Eastern Grey kangaroos congregate in smaller mobs. Generally, these include one dominant male with a modest harem of three or four females together with friends on the periphery that might include older sons of the family.

The gestation period for kangaroos is between 32 to 39 days.

## KINGFISHERS

It is believed that there are fewer than 6000 breeding pairs of kingfishers left in Britain because of the policy of allowing effluent to flow into rivers. House-building has caused many tributaries to silt up or they are covered over. However, in Australasia and in the Americas they still thrive.

The eggs of kingfishers are glossy white and depending on the species, the number of eggs they lay averages six. Both the male and the female take it in turn to incubate them.

## KIWI

Kiwi is an onomatopoeic word given by the Maoris because kiwi make the sound 'kiwi' when communicating. They are flightless birds found only in New Zealand and it is estimated that there are fewer than 70,000 specimens left.

Courting consists of the male kiwi strutting round the female grunting a lot. If he persists for long enough, she will eventually give in out of sheer boredom. The male strokes his mate with his long beak at the base of her neck. She bows forward and helps to accommodate him. The male is always much smaller than the female, so climbing onto her back is a question of balance. There is a good chance of fertilisation as a female kiwi has two distinct ovaries.

They mate for life. Some couples have been together for over 20 years. They share a burrow every third day or thereabouts, and when they get together they sing to each other. Male kiwi reach sexual maturity at 18 months, females are capable of breeding from 3 years old. They can survive for up to 60 years. In relation to its size, the kiwi lays the most enormous egg weighing a quarter of the mother's total weight.

The female kiwi can retain sperm in her body to fertilise her eggs as she sees fit. The first egg takes just over a month between mating and laying; the second egg a week less. They breed during the spring and the summer. Even kiwi brought to the northern hemisphere will time their breeding season to that of a New Zealand spring. Once the chick has fledged, the mother sends it on its lonely way to fend for itself. This is because until the advent of humans in New Zealand about a thousand years ago, the kiwi had no natural enemies.

The introduction of cats, dogs and stoats to New Zealand have done the most damage to the kiwi population. Efforts are being made to isolate kiwi in areas where they can establish their own territories and be safe.

## KOALAS AND WOMBATS

The word 'koala' comes from a defunct language of the aborigines meaning 'abstemious'. That is because you hardly ever see them drinking water. The koala is part of the Vombatiformes sub-order that also includes three species of wombat. They are marsupials, not bears, and they have opposable digits (two against three) like a chameleon. Females are larger than the male and their sexual appetite seems greater too. There have been frequent sightings of female koalas indulging in homosexual activities.

At the time of parturition, the baby is the size of a peanut. The mother takes this helpless little creature in her mouth and spits it into her marsupium (pouch). She has two teats and the youngster will attach itself to one of them. But mother koalas produce extremely small quantities of milk. After three months, the baby's eyes open and fur begins to grow. Six months later, it is strong enough to climb down to the ground and search for solid food. But before they are allowed to do that, the mother has a little surprise for them.

Baby koalas have a unique and in many ways an unenviable means of inoculation against diseases. The mother expels from her body a special type of faeces that the youngster has to eat from her cloacum. This pap is produced by the mother and eaten by the baby for about a month, resulting in some sort of immunisation, before devoting the rest of their lives to searching out and munching eucalyptus leaves – it needs over 2lb of leaves every night. Even so, there are so few energy calories in this diet that they need to sleep 20 hours daily. Perhaps because of this inactivity, they possess one of the smallest brains of all animals proportionally to their body. Koalas are not terribly bright.

They only come down to the ground in order to climb another gum tree.

During the breeding season (October to March), adult males bellow to attract the attention of females who respond with squeaks and screams. Whether or not the female is in oestrus, the male often forces himself onto the female, mounting her from behind. She has two vaginas. She frequently protests at the first attempt, and makes a noisy scene that draws the attention of other males in the vicinity. Fights between the males develop and in this way she is in a position to choose the strongest of the possible suitors. Once mounted, the male bites her neck and thrusts about 40 times in 20 seconds, ejaculating in both vaginas.

Koalas become sexually active after three years and their life expectancy is about 18 years.

## LEK

The *New Shorter Oxford English Dictionary* defines lek as: 'A patch of ground which the males of certain species of bird use solely for communal breeding displays and to which the females come to mate; such a gathering or display.' Lek is also used to describe similar rituals performed by other animals, such as the antelope. In this country, male black grouse, known as blackcock, are particularly noted for their competitive lekking displays.

## LEMURS

The International Union for Conservation of Nature (IUCN) has mooted that lemurs are the world's most endangered mammals, speculating that with the loss of habitat continuing at the present rate, they will be extinct by 2035. Native to Madagascar, the future of lemurs looks grim due to illegal logging and a succession of governments unwilling to legislate to protect them.

Lemurs are compensated for their colour-blindness by having an excellent sense of smell. They also have an armoury of places on their bodies to leave behind their scent and waft their pheromones. Male ring-tailed lemurs have scent glands on the inside of their forearms next to a spur with which they scent-mark tree branches. Most lemurs have scent glands on their scrotal skin. Others can leave behind reminders of themselves from the most private parts of their bodies.

They are social creatures that like to assemble in groups of 15 or so. Nocturnal species forage alone at night but come together with others to share nests during the day.

The mating season for lemurs has a narrow window of opportunity. Females are receptive for only three weeks a year, with their vaginas enlarging for no more than a few hours during that time. Their internal body clocks tell them what time do their mating so that the weaning periods are in synch with the season of highest food yields. With the approach of the mating season, scent-marking becomes all important. It is thought that the hormones contained in certain pheromones coordinate the timing of the females to come into oestrus simultaneously. Monogamous relationships exist within some species such as the red-bellied lemur and the mongoose lemur, but with others, polygamy is rife in the limited time that they have available.

The gestation period is about nine weeks for small species of lemur and as much as 24 weeks in larger lemurs. The latter generally give birth to one baby. It is common for the babies to ride on the backs of their mothers. There are certain species such as the bamboo lemurs that pick up the babies in their mouths and cart them around by the scruff of their necks as if they were kittens. Usually, both parents take it turns to groom and help feed the little ones.

Given the right conditions and an adequate food supply, lemurs can live for up to 30 years.

## LEOPARDS

The ancient Greeks thought leopards were a hybrid of lions and panthers. Hence the name: leo (lion) pard (panther). Some leopards are born black and these are called black panthers. It is the smallest of the four 'big cats' and is noted for its stealth and opportunism. It is easily identified by its fur, which is covered with black rosettes.

Leopards are solitary animals that prefer to prowl at night. They are excellent tree climbers and their preferred habitat is in wooded places. With logging and encroaching deforestation, they are being forced into the open.

In Siberia, leopards mate in January and February. The females seek out caves, crevices and hollow trees to make a den. After about three months, the female leopard gives birth to a litter of up to four cubs, born blind. They open their eyes at about a week old. After three months, the cubs accompany their mother when she goes hunting. At one year, the young leopards try hunting for themselves. They don't venture far from their mother's side until the age of two. It is estimated that nearly 50 per cent of the litter do not survive the first year. The lifespan of a leopard is typically between 12 and 17 years.

## LIONS

During the mating season, a pride of lionesses will keep their prospective male lion lovers in a perpetually concupiscent state. In oestrus, a lady lion can turn into a comparative nymphomaniac, and has been known to copulate more than150 times in the course of three days. If there is a paucity of lionesses, when a male lion feels randiness descending upon him, he will happily lie on his back and masturbate using his hind paws.

The gestation period for lions is between 105 to 113 days.

## LIZARDS

It is common in the animal world for a male to show off in front of the female in order to bolster his standing in her eyes. Birds preen themselves and humans breathe in deeply and throw out their chests. Male sagebrush lizards have developed a combination of the two. They push up on their forelegs to give themselves as much height as possible and then inflate their chests.

Whiptail lizards, native to Arizona, are all female. Scientists call them 'parthenogenetic unisexual pseudocopulators'. But that doesn't stop the ladies mounting each other and simulating sex. This is enough to induce the participant being stimulated into producing young that are carbon copies of herself.

## LLAMAS AND GUANACOS

The male llama, when feeling frisky, makes a sound in the back of his throat as if he is gargling. If the lady llama is up for it, she clucks rather like a turkey. They continue this dialogue while mating, which is not rushed and has been known to last more than an hour.

Llamas don't normally make much of a song and dance and live a placid existence. But when it is bedtime for baby llamas (called cria) the mother llama will hum a little lullaby – not particularly tuneful but a numbing sound that appears to put them to sleep.

## LOBSTERS

Until the mid-19th century, lobsters, like oysters, were looked down on as food for the poverty-stricken. Nowadays they are considered to be delicacies for the wealthy.

The lobster has 10 walking legs, and since they can live up to 60 years, this suggests that walking is good for you. In nature, their colour is a dark bluish-green. There is no humane way to kill lobsters. Throwing them in boiling water is illegal in parts of Italy, and in Reggio Emilia fines for so doing can be €500.

When a female lobster feels like having sex, she waits outside the male lobster's crevice or cave and, if he doesn't come out, she urinates into his space. The pheromones contained in her urine not only tell him what she wants him to know, but will arouse him hormonally. He staggers out half-swooning and watches her in a trance as she performs a provocative dance. He puts up a claw to tell her to desist but she slaps him down and places her claws on his head. He gives in easily and they enter his pad.

He watches while she sheds her shell, for she cannot mate with her carapace on. At length, she lies alluringly naked before him. Using his claws and mouth, he turns her onto her back. She yields softly as he inserts the hard front pleopods (also called swimmerets) that he normally reserves for swimming. His spermatophores (sacs of sperm) pass from his body into her seminal reservoir. And he hasn't even taken his boots off. The sperm remain in her seminal receptacle, which she can tap into at any time during the following two years. Exhausted and feeling famished after all that lovemaking, she snacks as well as she can on her discarded carapace. Then, overcome, she snuggles down in a corner of her beau's burrow for a week or so until a new shell has formed and hardened around her.

After she has recovered, she goes off for a bite to eat. When she finds a safe spot to raise a family she will fertilise her eggs – any number between 3000 and 100,000. After laying the eggs, they stay attached to the underside of her tail until they hatch about a year later. The resultant larvae float free and grub about on the seabed before evolving into tiny lobsters. Out of 100,000 eggs, only five on average will survive to adulthood.

## LOCUSTS (*SEE ALSO CICADAS*)

In the wild, locusts have a lifespan of three to five weeks. Too long!

## LORDOSIS

The *New Shorter Oxford English Dictionary* defines lordosis thus: 'A posture assumed by some female mammals during mating, in which the back is arched downwards; the assumption of such a posture.'

# M

## MANATEES AND DUGONGS

The sea cow should really have been called the sea elephant to whom it is related. Sea cows are also known as manatees and dugongs. Manatee is derived from a Carib word meaning 'breast' and Dugong is from Malay meaning (roughly) 'naughty lady of the sea'.

Female sea cows have large breasts like their elephant cousins. They also have prominent clitorises. Some of them (the Amazonians) have wavy manes. Add these physical attributes together and it becomes easier to understand why ancient mariners described them as mermaids.

When romping in warm water together, sea cows indulge in mutual masturbation and in these playful hours they tend to sing. As a result they are classed as *sirenians* and may have been the model on which those fateful 'sirens' were based in Greek mythology.

A female manatee reaches sexual maturity when she is about 5, whereas a male is not up to it until he is 9. When in oestrus, the female will be pursued by several males for some considerable time before she gives in and decides to mate. The males – up to a dozen of them – will rub themselves against the lady and try to kiss her, all the time emitting a high-pitched howl. She will mate with several of them before returning to her usual solitary existence.

Gestation lasts for over a year followed by another 18 months of weaning. On average she gives birth to one calf every three years. As soon as the calf is born, the mother brings it to the surface to breathe.

Manatees have a spoken communication with each other that no human has ever been able to decipher. They can live for up to 60 years. Their gentle, curious nature has made them vulnerable to the encroaching company of humans and ships and as such are designated an endangered species.

## MARSUPIALS

We tend to think of marsupials as kangaroos with joeys peeping out of their apron-pouches, or koalas, apparently half-stoned, staring at us from the branches of eucalyptus trees. They have anatomical differences from mammals that are not, at first sight, obvious. Their reproductive, intestinal and urinary tracts are all in one, and called cloacae, as in birds and reptiles.

There is a marsupial mouse that superficially looks identical to an ordinary European house mouse. It is called a Brown Antechinus, and it is nocturnal. The females, who do not possess pouches, build large communal nests because the babies must immediately attach themselves to their mother's teats – each female possesses eight.

The males only breed once, and that is enough for them. During the mating season, they do not stop to eat. All they want is sex. They go from one female to another, non-stop. Each coupling continues for up to 12 hours at a time. After two weeks of this, the male brown antechinuses will have developed suppurating ulcers, and their immune systems are so completely shattered that they are at the mercy of any disease or parasite in the vicinity. Within hours, every one of the males dies of exhaustion.

## MARTENS

Martens are small agile mammals that have a preference for coniferous woodland. They are omnivores and have bushy tails and large, retractable claws. Like dogs, they possess gristle in their penis to help them maintain an erection. They are solitary animals and live off mice and voles.

In early spring they give birth to litters of up to five kits – all born blind and hairless. They are weaned for three months after which they go into the woods and fend for themselves.

In Croatia and surrounding areas, until a couple of hundred years ago, the pelts of martens were used with which to barter in trade deals. Today, the Croatian word for marten, 'kuna', is the name of their currency.

Pine Martens, members of the weasel family, are about the size of domestic cats and they live in dens. They have litters averaging five kits, each of which weighs no more than 30gr at birth.

The Pine Marten holds its own against the gray squirrel and there is some optimism that martens will help to stop the decline of the red squirrel with whom it has no serious rival interest. In the wild, a Pine Marten typically lives for 10 years.

## MEERKATS AND MONGOOSES

There are 33 species of mongoose, and meerkats are one of the smaller sizes. They range over Asia and Africa. Their eyes have dark patches around them giving them the appearance of pirates with impaired vision. In fact, they can see better than humans, and a good thing too.

Meerkats spend their days browsing in the open for all the invertebrates they can eat, and as a bonus, should the opportunity arise, a small bird or two. Because it only weighs about 2lb, the meerkat is itself vulnerable to birds of prey.

But over the years of evolution, they have devised a system of lookouts. While the group is foraging, a sentry climbs to a high vantage point and keeps an eye open for danger. Should the guard spot a predator he lets forth a loud cry, coded to let the others know where the enemy is coming from – from the air or on foot. If it's an eagle, they do not hesitate, but as one they disappear down their air-raid shelters. If a ground-based animal is approaching, they run like the devil.

When they are courting each other, they giggle. When they mate they giggle even harder. Meerkats reach sexual maturity at one year of age. Before mating, there is no preening or display. The male grooms the female until one thing turns into another and they start to copulate. The male remains seated while the female takes things into her own hands.

The gestation period is 11 weeks and the cubs are born in the family burrow underground. The babies are totally dependent on their mother to begin with. Two weeks go by before their eyes open, and a few more days pass before their ears develop properly. They start to peek out of their burrows after three weeks but it takes up to two months to wean them.

Later, when the cubs emerge in order to learn how to forage, they are constantly accompanied by minders – older brethren or aunts – to rush them to safety should the need arise. The litter size is typically three; in the wild they may have four litters per year.

The dominant mating pair of any meerkat community are possessive enough to evict mothers with offspring that might stand as rivals to their own. When this happens, new meerkat communities develop, centred around the outcast family in which the mother may team up with a roving male. In the wild they have a lifespan of about seven years; in zoos they live twice as long.

## MICE

The meadow mouse (aka meadow vole – *Microtus pennsylvanicu*s) has a high mortality rate. In the wild it is lucky to survive 18 months. The mouse therefore dedicates a lot of its time to reproducing itself, as there is safety in numbers. The lady mouse begins to ovulate at the age of three weeks; the young male mouse starts producing sperm at seven weeks. Copulation is equally as important to them as eating. A female meadow mouse can produce 17 litters in a breeding season. This can add up to 100 babies per year. However, nearly 90 per cent of them die within a month. Even so, it is estimated that 100 pairs of voles – if they start breeding in April – could give birth to 8900 babies by September. The gestation period for mice is 19 to 31 days. Female mice are so promiscuous their litters are rarely the offspring of one father.

*Neonate* is the scientific term for an infant under four weeks old. Neonates of the Microtus group go through an interesting infancy. They are produced after their mother has passed the gestation period of around three weeks. The babies are pink and hairless and their eyes are shut. Within seven days they have a fully furred body and at that stage their eyes and ears open. They continue to wean for another week and after another two months, if they haven't fallen prey to birds, they will have achieved adult body weight. At about eight weeks, the male will start feeling frisky and will show great aggression to any other male who may have his eye on the same female.

Male mice tend to squeak in response to a female sending out her 'come-hither' pheromones. The squeaks are at such a high pitch that they are undetectable to the human ear. While mating, the males actually sing but again at such a high pitch that it takes special equipment to pick up the sound. The bush mouse eats protea at night when it blooms. This assists the protea to pollinate.

## MINK

Mink appear to enjoy a spot of sado-masochism as a preliminary to making love. They can indulge in foreplay for several hours, which is necessary in order to excite the female's ovaries.

Males vacate their dens and go on distant journeys hunting for mates. They may have many different sexual encounters during their odyssey. Like so many other animals mentioned in this book, the female mink has the curious ability to delay the gestation process following fertilisation. Normally, she could expect parturition after 39 days, but she is capable of putting everything in suspended animation up to 76 days before delivering her litter of 6 to 10 cubs and kittens. Young kits are weaned by 10 weeks and they leave to create dens of their own after three months. It takes another year before they are sexually mature.

The Animal Diversity Web tells us that there may be fewer than 30,000 European mink left in the wild. This is partly due to the accidental introduction of American mink to Europe. Both mink compete for the same food supply and the native species is outclassed by its American competitor.

## MOLES

The female mole has both ovaries *and* testicles. In the spring, the ovaries function normally after she has mated. Later in the year her testicles produce testosterone making her an aggressive defender of her burrow.

Richard Goolden (1895-1981), an English actor who was famous for playing the part of Mole in A A Milne's stage adaptation, *Toad of Toad Hall* (from Kenneth Grahame's *Wind in the Willows*), portrayed Mr Mole countless times between 1930 and 1979. On one occasion, in the seventies, Princess Margaret went to see a performance and afterwards asked the actor if he had changed his interpretation of the role over the years. Richard said, 'I recently read a book about moles. I discovered that after they have had sex, they fall into a steep decline and die. So now I play the part as a very old and virginal mole.'

(Whether Richard Goolden was correct in his assertion that moles decline and die following consummation of the sex act, I have not been able to discover. No doubt there will be readers of this book who can enlighten me.)

Moles have an enhanced sense of smell. This is necessary because they spend most of their time in the dark, underground. The female mole's sexy pheromones are enough for the male to make sure he finds her.

Trivia fact: there are no Irish moles.

## MOLLUSCS

There are at least 85,000 species of highly diverse molluscs comprising nearly 25 per cent of all marine organisms. Most molluscs have eyes and their minute brains encircle their oesophagus. All of them produce eggs that develop into trochophore larvae, although there are some that leapfrog the larvae stage and hatch directly into miniatures of their parents.

Anatomically, a mollusc has a small, fluid-filled cavity surrounding the heart, called the coelom. Surrounding the coelom are two gonads that deliver sperm or eggs (ova) into the coloem. Nephridiae (equivalent to the kidneys) extract the sperm or ova as if they were waste products and transfer them into the mantle cavity.

Prosobranchs have their gills, mantle cavity and anus situated in front of the heart. Prosobranch molluscs, including conches, cones, cowries, limpets, murexes, periwinkles, volutes and whelks spray sperm and ova into the water and allow luck to play a hand in fertilisation.

Other molluscs, such as mussels are hermaphrodites, and fertilise themselves internally. Timing of the spawning depends on the temperature and takes place between May and November.

Fresh water mussels give birth to larvae that live parasitically in the gills or on the fins of other fish for a few weeks until such time as they are sufficiently mature to drop off and live independently.

## CLAMS

Clams are bivalve molluscs, the largest of which are known as Giant Clams. They can live for a long time. A clam caught off the coast of Iceland in 2007 was believed to be well over 400 years old. In 1817, a clam was discovered off Sumatra that was four-and-a-half feet wide.

Giant clams are hermaphrodites: at certain times they are female, and at others male. They do not, however, self-fertilise (few animals do). Every clam has a primitive brain called a *cerebral ganglia* that incorporates a receptor area sensitive to something – yet to be faithfully analysed – called Spawning Induced Substance. Once this substance is released into the water, clams in the surrounding area immediately detect it and become sexually receptive. The clams will simultaneously release eggs and sperms. Once a year, the lady giant clam produces upwards of one thousand million eggs in a single burst, gushing like a geyser. Her reproductive urges continue for 30 or 40 years.

Other clams start to have muscle contractions, pumping water through their siphoning valves. Eggs and/or sperm are ingested and spawning begins. The timing of these spawnings is dependent on the moon cycle and the contractions, when they occur, take place every two or three minutes. These spawning sessions last anything from 30 minutes to two hours.

Fertilised eggs float freely until larvae hatch after 12 hours. Each larva automatically starts producing calcium carbonate to form a shell and after a few days it will have developed a 'foot' that it can anchor to the seabed.

Yes, and it's true: clams do it silently.

# MONKEYS

It's as well to remember that monkeys are the furry creatures with the tails. Apes, like their close relatives, humans, don't have tails (*see also Apes*). The gestation period for monkeys varies between 139 to 270 days. Here are a few tails of the monkey family:

After sexual intercourse, female baboons are so excited they can't stop chattering about it. The better the experience the more intense their pillow talk. The male baboons are buoyed by this and when baby baboons are born, the fathers are flattered enough to lend a hand.

The size of a lady baboon's rump indicates her worthiness as a potential mother – the more swollen it is the better.

Macaques seek secret hideaways when they have a date. Their reason is not modesty, Dutch biologists have decreed, but the fear of being seen by an alpha male who would interrupt and ruin the lovers' tryst. By the way, the so-called apes of Gibraltar are really macaques.

Marmosets are monkeys found in South America. They are generally small, typically 8ins (20cm) tall. They have claws rather than nails and are popular pets.

Marmosets exhibit 'germline chimerism' which occurs when the sperm and ova are not genetically identical to its own. Marmosets sometimes carry the reproductive cells of their fraternal twin siblings because of placental fusion that frequently results in producing fraternal twins, one of which is nearly always left to die.

Marmosets live high in the canopy of forests, chewing holes in trees and harvesting the gum inside. They live in family groups of up to 15, typically consisting of two breeding females, a few males with whom they share, together with other family members. The whole troop act as nannies to the children. They maintain a wide choice of sexual preferences, sometimes monogamous but more often they are into polyandry (an arrangement where a woman has two or more husbands at the same time).

Callicebus (or Titi) monkeys hail from South America. They are monogamous creatures. A male and a female will bond together, becoming fiercely protective of their territory. However, in some mysterious way, oestrus comes simultaneously to all the females. Faithfulness and boundaries fall by the wayside as the tribe of monkeys converge and indulge in a free-for-all sex-orgy. When the ladies' oestrus period fades away, the callicebus returns to its own territory and resumes a monogamous existence with its lifelong partner.

Titis live in trees and a typical family consists of two adults and five children. Mum and Dad show their affection for each other by twining their tails whenever the opportunity arises. The gestation period is five months. The babies are groomed equally by both parents, though the boy babies are taught to hunt by the father. They are fully grown at two years, and at 5 they go off to start a life of their own. Their life expectancy is 25 years.

Apart from twining tails, the characteristic for which titis are best known is their language. When in danger they whisper in a high-pitched manner. When at rest and to check that no other monkeys are moving too close to the boundaries of their territory, they emit a low-pitched howling that carries for miles.

# MONOGOMY

Monogomy amongst animals is not such an unusual situation as is popularly believed. This is a small selection of animals that mate for life.

Anglerfish
Barn owls
Bald eagles
Beavers
Black vultures
Brolga cranes
Condors
Coyotes
French angel fish
Gibbon apes
Golden eagles
Pigeons
Prairies voles
Prions
Ospreys
Red-tailed hawks
Sandhill cranes
Swans
Termites
Wolves
...and, er, Humans (sometimes)

# MOOSE (*SEE ALSO DEER AND ANTELOPE*)

Each year, the bull moose grows spectacular horns in readiness for the rutting season. Not only can he fight off rivals with these horns, they also act as ear trumpets. The hearing of a mature bull moose is 20 per cent better than the females or the junior moose. This enhanced sense enables the bull to hear the yearning cries of distant lady moose on heat.

## MOSQUITOES

*Mos-qui-toes, heaven forbid, do it,*
*So does ev'ry katydid do it...*

(lyrics by Cole Porter)

If amplified, the mating sound of a male mosquito would sound like a human wolf-whistle. Female mosquitoes flap their wings up to 500 beats per minute. Males are on the alert for the high-pitched buzz that results. They join the female in mid-air and the sex act, including the transfer of sperm to oviduct, is all over in 15 seconds.

## MOTHS (*SEE BUTTERFLIES*)

Like butterflies, moths are covered with dust-like scales that fall away if they are handled. Moth larvae such as the so-called bollworm are destructive to clothing, particularly wool, fur or silk.

In the fields, cotton, corn and tomatoes can be decimated by these Lepidoptera.

# N

## NAKED MOLE RATS

Naked mole rats are rodents who organise their life as if they were bees. They live entirely underground, digging burrows in search of root vegetables that they gnaw without quite killing them off. Here they form a troglodyte colony where a single alpha female lords it over the rest and reins as undisputed queen. She is attended by three males whose duty it is to take turns to service her. This male harem is attended by several hundred workers who have been delegated to act as nursemaids, larder guards and tunnel burrowers. These workers are sufficiently intimidated by the royal court to behave exactly as if they were eunuchs.

The queen has litters of 20 to 30 pups but she possesses only 12 nipples, so the babies have to take it in turn to suckle. A colony can survive for a quarter of a century before a new queen has to be chosen and crowned, by which time the displaced queen may have produced over 1000 offspring.

## NARWHALS

Big as they are, narwhals keep their mating habits private. They live in deep bays where there is an abundance of Arctic cod, Greenland halibut, squid, shrimp and cephalopods. Due to poorly evolved teeth, they apparently suck in most of their food.

Mating occurs in spring, usually around April. The calves are born 15 months later.

The males are competitive when love is in the air. Unlike the females, the male narwhal is equipped with a single long tusk on the top of its skull, which it uses as a weapon. Jousting takes place until either one of the tusks is broken or one of the combatants retires hurt. Males get the urge to do this at about 9 years old. It is believed that the legend of the Unicorn originated with early sightings of narwhals by ancient mariners.

The females are ready for mating at about 6 years old, and are capable of having one calf every three years. The calf stays with its mother for 20 months and in order for her to dive down deep and get a good feed, calves of a similar age group are occasionally herded into crèches under the supervision of a couple of aunties.

## NEWTS

Common newts are amphibians that divide their time between water and land. After winter hibernation they head for water in search of a mate.

The male newt has snazzy decorations on his toes, and along his back is a proud crest that he is only too willing to show off.

When he finds the lady of his dreams, he jigs and dances, and vibrates his tail, slapping it against his body to show how versatile he is. Then he throws down his sperm sac (his spermatophore) in a 'take it or leave it gesture'. She takes it and tucks it inside her body to fertilise her eggs.

Since the end of the Second World War, over a million ponds have vanished in Britain. The wetland habitats of newts have been destroyed and built on so that now the Great Crested Newt is becoming scarce.

The process whereby larvae change into grown newts is called metamorphosis. Once the female has deposited her eggs (somewhere in the region of 300) on an aquatic plant, the tadpole larvae, known as efts, begin to emerge after three weeks.

The larva at first has feathery outer gills, large eyes and an indeterminate shape. Twelve weeks later it has grown a longer body, a longer tail and its legs are well defined. By 16 weeks, it has become an adult newt.

## OCTOPUSES AND SQUID

The octopus has eight appendages called arms. They are sometimes incorrectly referred to as tentacles.

One of the arms is longer than the others and serves as a penis, but it does not eject sperm. It is known as a hectocotylus. A pair of octopuses in romantic mood will rub each other until their colour changes to a ripe, blushing hue. Then the male octopus uses his hectocotylus to reach into his breathing tube, which is where he keeps his sperm, and transfers these precious packets into his mate's mantel cavity with the aid of his ligula. This is a grasping hook at the tip of his penis arm.

Once the ligula has placed the sperm sac inside the female's mantle, the ligula breaks off and remains inside her. The octopus cannot regenerate this organ and the wound leads to his death a few weeks later.

Argonaut, or paper nautilus, is a weird species of octopus. First, they have a highly divergent sexual dimorphism. That's science-speak for the difference in body sizes between males and females. A female argonaut grows up to 4ins (10cm) with shells as large as 18ins (45cm). However, the male is only three-quarters of an inch (2cm) long!

His 'mating arm' detaches itself completely from his body and swims voluntarily into the much larger female octopus's cavity. The male, his duty done, is mortally wounded and swims away to die a lonely death.

Months later, when her eggs are ripe, the female takes the time to rip open the detached mating arm and spread the milt inside over her eggs to fertilise them. An Italian naturalist in the 1800s was the first to record sighting a detachable swimming penis. He mistook it for a parasitic worm.

Octopuses are allegedly highly intelligent – far more so than dogs. In Coburg, Germany, a captive octopus managed to squeeze out of his tank on several occasions, each time defusing the overhead lights by squirting jets of water at the lighting fitment.

In the Aegean sea lives a rare creature that, at first sight, looks like an octopus except that it has only six arms. This is known as a *hexapus*, and there have been fewer than five genuine sightings of the animal.

## OESTRE

Oestre was the Anglo-Saxon Goddess of Spring and Fertility (sometimes spelt Eostre – from which the word Easter is derived. In Germany, the month of April is known as *ostermonat*).

The Venerable Bede (673-735) in his work 'De Temporum

Ratione' related how on one particular occasion a songbird flew down and sat on Oestre's hand. Oestre, conscious of her responsibilities as a fertility goddess, transformed the bird into a rabbit.

The rabbit was unhappy because however much he hopped, he couldn't fly. The children begged Oestre to change the bunny back into a bird but Oestre could only do so when her power was strongest in the spring, and they all had to wait until then before the rabbit was turned back into a bird and started laying eggs again.

## OESTRUS

The *New Shorter Oxford English Dictionary* defines Oestrus as: 'The period of a female animal's readiness to mate, accompanied by certain physiological changes; the rut, heat.' In common parlance, this is usually referred to as the time an animal is 'on heat'. In animals, a signal trait of oestrus is the 'lordosis reflex', in which there is an instinctive reaction by the female to elevate her hindquarters.

## OPOSSUMS

The Virginian opossum is an American marsupial – colloquially called a 'possum' – and is generally a nocturnal creature that grows to the size of a large house cat. There are up to 66 species of the family Didelphidae. It prefers to make its den in a hollow tree. If confronted by what it considers to be insuperable odds it will lie on the ground pretending to be dead, hence the expression 'playing possum'.

The male possum has a bifurcated penis and the female has two uteri. The boys are called jacks and the girls are called jills.

The jills are capable of conceiving more than 20 babies at a time. The young, born a couple of weeks after fertilization, are blind, naked and grublike, weighing only 2 grams (0.07 ounce). They have to grasp their way with their forepaws through the mother's hair from the birth canal up to the pouch wherein the nipples are hidden. Though not definitely understood, it is believed that the tiny blind embryonic-looking creatures find their way to the milk through their sense of smell.

Female possums can have litters numbering up to 13 pups three times a year. However, any pups above that number are unlikely to survive, as each mother possesses a mere 13 teats.

## ORCHIDS (THE ANIMAL VARIETY!)

You are perfectly right – orchids are not animals. Not yet anyway. But certain orchids shape themselves to look like wasps and bees. They can mimic the real thing so well that the wasps and bees concerned are fooled into simulating mating with the orchid. The flower's pollinia (a mass of coherent pollen grains) can then be carried off by the insect to pollinate elsewhere.

## OSTRICHES AND EMUS

These flightless birds have flat breast bones and their wings have shrunk to a vestigial form following thousands of years of disuse. Ostriches live in South Africa; Emus settled in Australia.

Once upon a time, there was a continent called by geologists Gondwana. Over millions of years, the Earth split into separate parts and some of the animals evolved in Africa and some in Australia. So all we know for certain is that about 80,000,000 years ago, emus and ostriches shared a common ancestor.

Ostriches grow quickly. By the age of six months they are nearly as tall as their parents – 7ft to 10ft high. They are the only bird in the world with two toes. Emus, not quite so big, take longer to develop – they aren't fully grown until the age of two, but they have the standard three toes. Both types of bird have exchanged the benefits of flight for the sheer exhilaration of running extremely fast. They have developed into superb runners and can easily maintain 30 miles per hour.

They are sometimes farmed for their meat; their hides are used for leather, their feathers for fashion and their eggs as ornaments. Privately, I suspect they wish they hadn't been created to look so cute.

Ostriches breed at between three to four years of age. Emus start at 18 months. The males of both species incubate the eggs. Ostrich eggs hatch after six weeks; emu eggs hatch after seven weeks.

During the Australian summer months, December to January, emus form breeding pairs, stake out their territory and stay together for six months. They wait until it's cooler in May or June before actually mating. As the big moment approaches, the testicles of the males double in size. The feathers of the females change into a richer hue and the skin around their eyes turns blue as if they have been overusing the eye shadow. The females do all the courting, provocatively swinging their hips as they circle the mate of their choice whilst calling out in seductive chirrups reminiscent of a snare drum. The male watches transfixed as she continues to shuffle around him, keeping her eyes directed towards him and at the same time waggling her tail feathers in his direction. Her cloaca swells.

Eventually, he gets the message and approaches her tentatively as she leads him on a pretty dance into a shady spot. If a female has lured a male already spoken for, the incumbent female can get really mad and a catfight breaks out. The males look on resignedly and so as not to waste time while the girls are kicking each other, they build a rough nest of twigs and grass in readiness for the clutch of eggs that they are confident of fertilising with one female or another.

When it comes to the point of making sexual contact, the male fans out his feathers and pecks the ground, sidling closer to the female. Then he extends his neck and sways his head from side to side, rubbing his chest against the female's posterior.

Emus nest when the weather is coolest and they continue mating every other day. Every third day – on average – she lays an egg until the clutch accumulates to around 11 eggs. These are dark green and on average 5ins long. The shells are at least a millimetre thick. While his mate is busy laying these tough eggs, the male gets broody and once the clutch is complete it is the male who pushes in on top of them and incubates the eggs. Until the eggs are hatched, the male neither eats nor drinks. Indeed, he only stands up to turn the eggs over – a process that he goes through with military precision 10 times every day. The incubation period continues for 56 days during which time the male emu loses over a third of his body weight.

Meanwhile, the female may mate with other males and have separate clutches in new nests. Mothers may visit their various broods as they begin to hatch, but otherwise, household chores are left to the male. Cleverly, he increases the temperature before the last hatchlings are due to emerge so that the eggs, although laid sequentially, will hatch within three or four days of each other. The 5-inch chicks are fully formed and leave the nest after a few days. The father stays with them for nearly three-quarters of a year until such time as they are ready to make their own way in the world. Until then, the father is aggressively protective, covering his chicks with his feathers every night and shooing off all other animals and emus. Even their mother gets short shrift from the fussy father, not that she's bothered. In the wild, emus can achieve a life span of 20 years.

## OTTERS

Otters are part of a large family that includes badgers, polecats, weasels and wolverines. The word 'otter' comes from the same Indo-European language that gave us 'water'. From this, we may deduce that otters live on or near water. They are playful creatures, creating waterslides for themselves and generally having a splashing good time.

They live in dens that we call 'holts'. It is difficult for them to keep their holts private and pretend they are not at home, since the smell of their faeces is distinctive, sometimes described as akin to rotten fish. This tell-tale sign is known as spraint.

Otters lead a respectable family life. Females reach sexual maturity at two, males get there a year later. The gestation period is from 60 to 86 days. A newly born puppy is pampered by its mother, father and older brothers and sisters. After a couple of months, the pup ventures out for swimming practice although it always returns to the holt to live amongst the family for at least another year. The lifespan of otters is 16 years.

# OWLS

*The most sedate barnyard fowls do it,*
*When a cockerel cries.*
*High-browed old owls do it,*
*They're supposed to be wise...*
(LYRICS BY COLE PORTER)

Owls get together in the spring and try timing the forthcoming rearing of hatchlings to fit in with the supply of prey available in their territory.

A male owl will t'wit and immediately a female owl will respond with a t'woo. If the response is good, the male will guide the female to a pre-fabricated nest site – often the abandoned nest of some other bird. He will then tempt her with a tasty bite of vole or mouse. If she accepts, his next move is to mate with her and their consummation is sealed with a cloacal kiss. Some owls, like the Little Owl, stick together for a year. Others, such as the Tawny Owl, mate for life. All owls, particularly Great Greys and Tawnys protect their nests with ferocity. People have lost eyes by venturing too close.

Owls can lay up to a dozen eggs at a time, although three or four is the more common number. Incubation goes on for a month. Like a crocodile, the chick inside the egg is equipped with an 'egg tooth'. With this, he chips his way out of the shell and into the world, and his mother will keep him warm while the father feeds him and any other chicklings up to 10 times a day. After another five weeks, the chicks venture out of the nest and survey their territory from a safe height. At this stage of their development they are known as 'branchers'. They remain here for another month until they become confident enough to learn to fly. And now they are fledglings.

It takes another year or sometimes two before these owlets are old enough to breed and start their own families.

A tawny owl can live to 18. A Great Horned Owl can get to 50, depending on the local predators. But for most owls, to attain the age of 10 is as much as can be hoped for.

It is estimated that there are fewer than 4000 pairs of Barn Owls left in Britain. Intensive farming has affected their habitat. Their nesting trees have been felled and many die at nights in collision with traffic.


## OYSTERS

The oyster is a bi-valved mollusc. Its name derives from the Latin word, *Ostrea*, meaning bone or shell.

It has recently been discovered that oysters contain rare amino acids that may be linked to the reproductive process, so the old wives' tale regarding the sexual potency that a man might achieve from swallowing these creatures may have a grain of truth in it. Those old wives knew a thing or two, and probably still do. The particular amino acids are at their height in the spring during the oysters' breeding season. They make their permanent homes on stony sea bottoms varying from 9ft to 60ft in depth.

An oyster (as well as any well endowed mussel) can lay hundreds of thousands of eggs a year. The males discharge sperm into the water and pray for a lucky hit. However, they are known as 'alternating hermaphrodites'. This means that if they are not getting much feedback in their male personae, they can transform themselves into females and become receptive partners. The genital openings on either side of their body can at one time produce ova and at another spermatozoa. This ensures that an oyster cannot fertilise itself. An inbred oyster might turn out to be really stupid.

When an oyster is in its female state and producing eggs, fishermen call this part of the cycle as being in a 'white spat'. The ejected ova float near the surface, absorbing the sun and mixing with free floating milt (sperm) and gradually become tiny embryos. At a certain stage of development they sink to the bottom and attach themselves to a hard surface to begin their life cycle as oysters. They grow at the rate of about one inch in diameter per year and can live for up to 20 years, although their average life span is about 10 years.

# PANDAS

Cuddly pandas, with faces like liquorice allsorts, are really a type of mountain bear but they have become very lazy over the years. They detest physical exercise, don't do much mountain climbing and if they are not eating, they sleep. They are native to China and achieve a height of around 3ft. It is estimated that there are fewer than 2000 pandas living today, with about a sixth of these survivors in captivity.

Female giant pandas are receptively fertile for only a couple of days each year. This window of sexual opportunity is so narrow that some male pandas have missed the boat entirely. They've been known to neglect getting on with their important contribution to breeding by sleeping right through it. In captivity, things can be worse. Pandas learn by watching their elders but animals in zoos have no other pandas to set the example. Therefore, some pandas simply don't know how to have sex.

David Wildt, the head of the Centre for Species Survival at the National Zoo in Washington DC has had problems with his two pandas, Tian Tian (the male) and Mei Xiang (the female). They go through the pre-sex ritual with flying colours. She wanders around her enclosure, scent-marking various surfaces with a waxy, hormone-rich emission from a gland near her vulva. She might even walk through water to spread her pheromones far and wide. Her vocalisation changes to that used by female pandas to indicate they are not going to play coy should a lusty male attempt intimacy. She may even masturbate to keep those pheromones coming. She does all that a panda can do to solicit the male's attention. But then, apparently, things go pear-shaped. Tian Tian is hovering in her vicinity, looking quite interested. But Mei Xiang does not present herself in the proper position for copulation. She assumes what David Wildt has called 'the pancake position' – she spreads herself out on her stomach with legs outstretched, waiting for something to happen. Tian Tian, unworldly in these respects, stands astride Mei Ziang looking down with the expression of a panda who would like to do something really interesting but who doesn't know what that something is. This is all most frustrating for the keepers, let alone the pandas.

The National Zoo regularly monitors the female's hormone levels. Volunteers watch Mei Ziang day and night, noting where she has left scent marks so that keepers can take samples. When the big once-a-year-day arrives, the scientists are ready for action. There is a permanent arrangement for a Chinese consultant to be on stand-by, ready to fly in at short notice: all to no avail. Artificial insemination has been tried two or three times but the cubs have not survived for long. To extract the semen, a probe is inserted into the male's rectum and a low voltage switched on, which leads to an electro-ejaculation.

Initially, the National Zoo paid China $1million a year to rent the pair of pandas. Three other American zoos have pandas: San Diego, Memphis and Atlanta. The San Diego pandas seem to have got the hang of sex and are reproducing their species satisfactorily. Other zoos with pandas (whose breeding programmes are only meeting with limited success) include those in Australia, Austria, Canada, France, Japan, Mexico, Singapore, Spain, Taiwan, Thailand and the United Kingdom.

Conditions must be perfect, including lots of straw to play roly-poly, an ambient temperature and complete darkness. The last of these conditions adds to the difficulty experienced by observers trying to witness exactly how pandas get it on. The amount of daylight to which they are exposed is critical in its effect on their hormonal state – a fact that has, hitherto, made breeding in captivity, extremely difficult.

When a female panda reaches the age of six she will start to ovulate. The period of 'being in heat' is known in biology as the oestrous cycle. This occurs once a year in springtime when the rainy season is over. Her vulva changes colour and turns bright red. She becomes relatively frisky by hurrying around nuzzling the tails of male pandas, splashing about in water, chattering in an excited fashion and pretending to be coy by bending over whilst covering her eyes with her paws. If this doesn't work, she may resort to urinating against a tree stump in the hope that wafting her pheromones might attract a gentleman's attention.

The male panda sometimes leaves a token of his urine on a nearby tree trunk, which can act like a magnet to a female on heat. His wrist bones have developed something like an extra thumb that enable him to climb down trees head-first. He has been known to wee on the trunk just as his head nears ground level. This possibly encourages the female to think he is a very tall and virile bear.

Pandas are usually solitary animals so the female is lucky if she finds a male partner in the vicinity. However, though the mating season is short, most males under the age of 20 are keen enough to have a fling and they will service more than one panda should the opportunity present itself. Should there be several male pandas in the offing, they will go through the motions of fighting for the hand of the damsel. Pandas are not up to a lot of physical stuff though. Fisticuffs is out. A bit of pushing and snarling is as far as it goes.

When he gets round to the sexual act, the male panda mounts the female from behind, but copulation lasts for less than five minutes. Afterwards, the fellow, unused to such exertion on this scale, will wander off and continue his bachelor-like existence, having a kip before searching for the next meal of bamboo. To maintain his lifestyle, he eats at least 30lb of bamboo every day. He is not territorial and he seems totally disinterested in his offspring. Eating and sleeping fills this mountain bear's entire existence.

The female panda, on the other hand, builds a den and stakes out her territory. Her pregnancy goes through two stages. The fertilised egg divides into a primitive, incomplete embryo and for the first two months floats freely inside the amniotic fluid of its mother's womb. At some point the embryo attaches itself to the uterine wall and proper development takes place over a further two months.

At birth, a panda cub is the smallest of all mammals, with the exception of some newborn marsupials. It weighs barely five ounces, is hairless and does not open its eyes until it is five weeks old. It takes a few weeks for this embryonic shape to develop into a recognisable panda. It attempts to crawl after two-and-a-half months. The mother is only capable of raising one cub at a time so if she has given birth to twins, one of them is left to die.

Red pandas are not actually pandas at all (*see Red Pandas*).

## PARASITES

It is outside the scope of this book to take a peek at the lives of parasitic microbes, but there is one called *taxoplasma gondii* that has such an extraordinary life cycle that it is worth a mention here.

The taxoplasma parasite can only reproduce inside the intestines of cats although as a multihost parasite it can live in any mammal. It exists in the human body and many people have it inside them with no ill effects. On the other hand, if you are old or poorly, the little microbe seems to realise your vulnerability and takes advantage.

The way it reproduces is this. When a member of the feline family is infected, usually by eating an infected mouse, the parasite settles down in the cat's small intestine where it becomes sexually mature and reproduces millions of *oocysts* – in layman's terms this means countless baby microbe parasites. The next step is for the microbes to venture out into the world by hitching a ride in the cat's faeces. For this reason it is advisable that pregnant women should avoid changing cat litter.

A cat's faeces can go places – it can be caught on the skin of a human or the hair of a dog, or more often than not, sent to a rubbish dump to be consumed by rats or mice. However, to complete its lifecycle, the microbe must get back into a cat again to reproduce.

Mice, wisely, have an innate fear of cats. The merest whiff of cats' urine will send sensible mice scampering back to their holes. But a mouse infected with the parasite toxoplasma will induce the opposite effect. In ways yet to be explained, the microbes programme a mouse's brain to lose its fear and, instead, to be pally with his fiercest enemy. Infected mice might as well go up to cats and say 'eat me'. Unfortunately for the mice, that is exactly what cats do. Once inside a cat, toxoplasma starts its lifecycle again and reproduces itself a million-fold.

## PARROTS, MACAWS AND COCKATOOS

The plumage of parrots contain an ultra violet fluorescence that cannot be seen with the human eye, though to a parrot, the feathers flash enticingly like the neon lights round Times Square. The gaudier the sexier. Not that parrots are promiscuous. For the most part, once parrots have chosen their partner, they remain faithfully bonded for life. It is not so unusual amongst birds to stick together with a special mate. Others that are usually monogamous include doves, swans, geese, most hawks, eagles, falcons, albatrosses and ravens.

The Grey Parrot, also known as the African Grey Parrot is

considered by experts to be one of the most intelligent birds in the world. In the wild as dusk falls, grey parrots appear to talk to each other before going to sleep. They repeat all the sounds they have heard during the day. Because of its gentle nature and ability to mimic practically anything, it has proved popular as a pet. As a result, many have been captured from the wild and shipped to Europe in inadequate crates before being sold on to pet shops, many of the birds dying en route. CITES (the Convention on International Trade in Endangered Species of Wild Fauna and Flora) has restricted such transactions because the wild population was proving to be unsustainable.

The lifespan for one of Australia's largest parrots, the cockatoo, is typically 65 years. The macaw doesn't fall off his perch until he has reached 50.

## PEAFOWL

These birds' original home was in India. The males are known as peacocks, the females are peahens and the babies are peachicks. They sleep in trees, so they are capable of flight, although they are reluctant to do so in front of admirers. They make their nests on the ground.

The eyes in the huge fan of a peacock's tail are known as the oceli. Peacocks give a great display to attract a mate's attention – spreading and vibrating their tail feathers – making a sound like the rustle of leaves in a spring breeze. Fickle peahens go after the peacock with the most oceli.

The mating call of a peacock has often been mistaken for the scream of a woman. They are good guards, ready to make a clamour if something disturbs their territory. Humans frequently employ them for this ability and the warning call of a peacock can sound like a dog barking.

## PENGUINS

*Penguins in flocks, on the rocks, do it,*
*Even little cuckoos, in their clocks, do it*
(LYRICS BY COLE PORTER)

Penguins really like sex. They live in a freezing cold region and if there's anything that can take their mind off the weather, it's the mating game. They're not promiscuous, they find a partner and bond for life – or at least for the duration of that breeding season – but once they are together they're very fond of sex.

There are 16 types of penguin. They are, in alphabetical order: Adélie, African, Chinstrap, Emperor, Erect-crested, Fiordland, Galapagos, Gentoo, Humboldt, King, Little, Macaroni, Megallanic, Rockhopper, Snares, and Yellow-eyed. Each type has its own way of life and has evolved its own method of survival, and I will try to describe the routine of just one, the Emperor Penguin, the biggest of them all, and indeed the penguin with one of the most bizarre lifestyle.

They walk from the edge of the ice pack up to 70 miles to reach their Antarctic nesting areas in late March or early April while it is still bitter winter (minus 40 degrees centigrade).

The male places his head on his chest before giving a courtship call. He repeats this until his ex-wife, if she is still living, or some new lady who responds to the call, comes to stand in front of him face-to-face. Like reflections in a mirror, they mimic each other's movements for some minutes. Satisfied with what they see, they find a segregated spot. The female makes a deep bow, her bill almost touching the ground. He nods and does the same himself. Then he will stand behind his chosen mate and vibrate his wings against her back. Some observers call this 'flipper patting' but it seems like heavy petting to a penguin. She lies down and the male will mount her from behind. She obliges him by flipping her tail sideways, exposing her cloaca.

As in most birds, penguins have no external genitalia. The male's sperm is produced in the testes and stored in his cloaca (*see Cloaca*). This is an all-purpose orifice for defecating, urinating, and reproduction. The female also has a cloaca that leads to the ovaries. Once the female penguin is lying flat on the ground with her flippers out to keep her stabilised, the male penguin presses his cloaca onto hers and passes the sperm through, assisting their passage with a little wriggle of his tail. This is 'The Cloacal Kiss' in a cold climate. During the encounter, he caresses her neck with his beak, but it doesn't last long. The ground is too cold to lie on for much longer than a minute, so copulation is hardly an experience to savour. Positioning himself on top of her is not easy for the male penguin and observers have noted that the chances of his falling off her are high. However, if at first they don't succeed, penguins are only too happy to try and try again.

By early June, her egg is laid, weighing about 1lb. The female Emperor Penguin transfers it very carefully to her mate and rests it on top of his feet, for if the egg were to touch the ice, it would freeze and die. The cock bird keeps the egg warm by tucking it under a large fold of skin until it hatches. The female scuttles off to the sea to feed, leaving the male without food for about two months. She is gone so long because her trek to the sea can be up to 70 miles.

The males huddle together in large groups to conserve body heat in the harsh environment, where winds can reach up to 120mph (200kph). They take it in turns to get into the centre of the huddle where the wind is less harsh. After 64 days, the egg hatches, a process that takes three days. The father feeds the chick with a protein substance produced by a gland in his oesophagus.

When the female returns, she finds her mate (and chick) by listening out for one particular bugle call over thousands of others. By this time, the male will have lost about 44 pounds in weight. The father waddles off to the sea to break his fast, and may be away for three or four weeks. On his return they share the responsibilities of rearing the chick. Two months later the chicks are herded together into a crèche where thousands of birds are packed tightly together as mutual protection against the cold. Unfortunately, 80 per cent of Emperor Penguin chicks do not survive their first year.

Female chinstrap penguins play a game of catch-me-if-you-can with their chicks. When it's time for tea in the penguin crèche, the mother will frequently run away, forcing her baby to run after her. If the chick is not capable of keeping up, it will eventually die of starvation – a sad example of the survival of the fittest.

The macaroni penguins take it in turns to sit on their egg. They have usually prepared a little nest of stones and twigs and it takes about a month for the baby to hatch. Mum and Dad take turns in caring for their offspring.

## PHEASANTS AND GROUSE

The Common Pheasant (called the Chinese Pheasant in the US) is widespread throughout the world. It originated in Asia and over the years has been introduced elsewhere as a game bird. It is reared by gamekeepers to be shot for sport.

Pheasants are gullible creatures, only too ready to breed if the right conditions are provided for them. Generally when mating, they form a breeding pair that remains together for the season. Occasionally, a male can have a small harem under his roost.

They present easy targets for the gun-toting community. They are 2ft to 3ft long and their body plumage is a mixture of bright gold and brown with green, purple and white markings. Under their beaks hangs a red wattle, set against a white neck ring.

Grouse are of the same order of birds as chickens, though they couldn't be mistaken for each other, unless you can imagine chickens in fancy dress. Grouse have feathered nostrils and feathers right down to their toes to keep their feet warm. Unlike chickens, they have no spurs on the backs of their ankles.

As hatchlings they eat worms, grubs and insects but as they grow into adulthood, they become herbivorous. They are social animals and, inside their territory, flocks of a hundred birds can live together.

With the exception of the Willow Ptarmigan, male grouse are polygamous. Come the breeding season, at sunrise and dusk, the males can be seen showing off in courtship displays, the females watching from the designated courting area (leks).

The males sport their brightly-coloured combs, display their plumage like models on a catwalk and inflate the impressive Technicolor sacs on their necks. All this time, they sing, shout, cluck and even bark like a dog in an attempt to get a response from their audience. If their cabaret falls on deaf ears, the males resort to drumming with their feet, rattling their tails and, as a last resort, taking off and giving a hedge-hopping flying display.

They nest in shallow depressions in the ground, hiding as far as possible amongst vegetation. After mating, it takes only a week before the female lays her clutch – typically six to 12 eggs – spread over a few days. They are the same size as hens' eggs but their colour is pale yellow with brown polka dots. The female takes three to four weeks to incubate them. When the chicks emerge, they are thickly covered in yellow-brown down. They are able to leave the nest on the spot and start pecking about for insects. Both parents keep a protective eye on them. Within two weeks the nestlings are fledged and thereafter they fly to another part of the territory.

The Willow Ptarmigan – or Red Grouse – is the state bird of Alaska. It has a fairly wide habitat across the forests and moorlands of most of Northern Europe. It nests in the spring and the chicks behave like any other grouse species.

One peculiarity of Willow Ptarmigans is their complete change of plumage for the winter months. From a marbled-brown colour, both sexes turn completely white, except for their black tail feathers. Unlike other grouse, the male Willow Ptarmigans are faithfully monogamous. This trait leads to a great deal of possessiveness, which in turn, can be the cause of a lot of fighting between males. The father helps his mate rear their chicks, and he seems to take a pride in his family.

## PHEROMONE

Pheromone is a word you will encounter frequently throughout this book. The *New Shorter Oxford English Dictionary* definition is: 'A chemical secreted and released by an organism which causes a specific response when detected by another organism of the same (or a closely related) species.'

## PIGEONS AND DOVES

The female pigeon is programmed by nature to be incapable of laying eggs without another pigeon in the vicinity. Pigeon fanciers, aware of this fact, place a mirror in the pregnant pigeon's loft. Seeing her own reflection is reassurance enough for the bird to trigger the process of egg-laying. Both male and female pigeons secrete crop milk after mating in preparation for feeding chicks.

## PIGS

When mating in the wild, a guinea pig ejaculates a large amount of semen into the sow's vagina, which quickly coagulates into a solid plug. This ensures not only that no sperm is lost, but also it blocks the female's passage, deterring any rival from becoming a lusty wooer.

The domestic pig is descended from the wild boar and started its journey to farmyard animal about 12,000 years ago, probably in the Tigris River basin. The natural proclivity of pigs is to make a nest and change the bedding frequently to keep it clean. Unfortunately, farmed animals are not often given the opportunity to do so. Forced to live in squalor, we call them 'dirty pigs' when all they really want is straw and a suitable area away from their nest to deposit their excreta. Pigs are highly intelligent and can learn tricks and behaviour patterns as well as, if not better than, any dog. Their wonderful sense of smell makes them ideal for snuffling out truffles, a delicacy on the continent.

Sows come into oestrus from eight months old, and after that it occurs regularly every 21 days. The boar is ready to breed at 10 months old and the mating process takes about 15 minutes. Without outside intervention, he is capable of servicing three sows each day. The gestation period lasts 115 days.

When a sow is nearly ready to give birth, she and her partner will dig out a hollow about the same size as her body. This she lines with grass and straw, twigs and leaves, carrying her bedding materials by mouth until she has a comfortable mound to lie on. She covers this with sticks except for a small hollow in the middle where she intends to give birth. Then she lies on her side in this hammock and waits for parturition.

Suckling occurs once an hour. The piglets soon learn that there is a 'teat order' – with the runt of the litter getting the richest milk. A virgin female pig is called a gilt.

## PLATYPUSES

Platypuses are one of the last surviving examples of a crossover animal in the evolution from reptiles to mammals. Although classed as a mammal it is also a monotreme. Originally, Australians settlers called it a duckmole.

When it was first discovered, scientists considered it to be a gigantic hoax. In 1798, a naturalist named Dobson submitted a dried specimen of a platypus to the British Museum for examination. Dr George Shaw described the finding as 'of all the Mammalia yet known ... the most extraordinary in its conformation; exhibiting the perfect resemblance of the beak of a Duck engrafted on the head of a quadruped'. To this day, the marks made by the scissors that Shaw used to check that the beak had not been stitched on are still visible. It was widely suspected at the time that this extraordinary animal had been mocked-up by an Asian taxidermist.

The platypus has a duck's bill, waterproof fur, a beaver's tail, webbed feet and it lays eggs. The male platypus has extra retractable claws on his hind feet that can scratch, leaving venom in the wound of the victim. The poison can cause severe pain and illness in humans, and with smaller animals such as dogs, the scratch can be lethal.

Its body temperature is five degrees lower than in comparable placental mammals. Monotremes are the only mammals to lay eggs instead of giving birth to live young. Another unique feature is that apart from dolphins, platypuses are the only animals known to locate their prey by electroreception. These detectors, sensitive to the minutest electrical currents are situated in the animal's bill. The senses of sight, smell and hearing are irrelevant to a platypus when it is hunting for food, because on diving underwater, it closes its eyes, ears and nose. In the wild, its life expectancy is 11 years.

It was not until 1884 that confirmation came through that platypuses lay eggs. A young Cambridge naturalist, W H Caldwell, was sent out on an expedition to find more about monotremes (platypus and echidna) and whether they really lay eggs, which was rumoured but generally disbelieved. Caldwell recruited 150 aborigines and eventually they found some eggs. The long debate about whether platypuses laid eggs or not was resolved. In a famous telegram sent to the British Association for the Advancement of Science meeting in Canada in 1884, Caldwell wrote: 'Monotremes oviparous, ovum meroblastic.' In layman's terms this translates as 'monotremes lay eggs of the same sort as reptiles'.

Their breeding system typically occurs between June and October. It is thought that females become sexually active in their second year and continue to mate until the age of 10. They are considered polygynous.

The males live in their own burrows and rarely come out except to hunt and breed. However, the female constructs an elaborate burrow for her future family. This tunnel, close to water and generally a foot higher than the water level, has been known to be at least 60ft in length and with many side turns that can be quickly blocked off in the event of flooding or being chased by a predator. She lines her nesting area with leaves for bedding material, carrying materials under her tail.

The female has two ovaries but only the left ovary is functional, probably an evolutionary process between reptile and mammal. Approximately 28 days following fertilisation, she lays a clutch of two eggs (or occasionally three) that appear to be completely spherical. She sits on the eggs for 10 days, by which time the embryonic platypus has developed an 'egg tooth' to peck his way out of the shell.

Newly hatched platypuses are blind and hairless and rely on their mother's milk which, in the absence of teats, exudes through the skin of her stomach into tiny grooves from which the youngsters can lap it up. Suckling the babies in this fashion continues for about four months. Thereafter the young platypuses are capable of foraging along with their mother. They are born with milk teeth

– three-cusped molars – but they lose these early on and develop keratinized plated pads with which to grind their food.

## POLAR BEARS

Polar bears have black skin under their translucent hair. The females reach sexual maturity at the age of 6; the males at around 7. However, few male polar bears mate before they are 9 years-old. They breed on the sea ice between April and May.

The Inuit refer to the polar bear as 'Nanook'. This bear, one of the largest carnivores, lives on the ice but rarely ventures further north than 88 degrees. It is estimated that there are 25,000 of them. They prefer to keep to the edge of ice packs close to the open sea where they can follow the migration of their favourite meal – the seal. Their olfactory senses are so sensitive that they can smell a seal a mile away. They can survive without food for over three months. They do not hibernate.

Polar bears are insulated with blubber – four inches deep – under their fur. In April and May they converge at the places where seals are likely to turn up looking for fish. While waiting for them to arrive the males often fight with each other for the possession of a possible mating partner and they can sustain severe wounds. There are generally three male polar bears competing for one female. Once the dominant male has won his prize he and the sow will stay together and mate repeatedly for a week or more. Consummation results in ovulation in the sow.

During her lifetime the female polar bear may produce four or five litters. After mating, the fertilised egg remains in a suspended state in the same way as with the grizzly, except that there is no true hibernation to follow. During the four months until September, the pregnant sow eats copious amounts of food, gaining at least 440lbs (200kg).

Before winter sets in, the sow finds a snowdrift on the ice somewhere near the edge of the sea. She digs a cave in the snow and in this hollow, protected from the freezing winds, she rests through the winter, only venturing out on clear days when she might be able to find food. As winter comes to a close, she gives birth to her cubs, in anticipation of the spring season.

In a similar way to martens and dogs, bears have gristle in their penises that assists erection in cold weather. Very handy if you live in the Arctic.

## POLYANDRY

The *New Shorter Oxford English Dictionary* describes polyandry as, 'The fact or state of a female animal having more than one male mate.'

## PORCUPINES

Female porcupines come into (hymeneal) heat only once a year, and then for less than six hours. The lady will indicate her readiness by rubbing her genital area against nearby objects, leaving tell-tale pheromones in the air. When the tiny, four-legged male gets the message, he stands on his hind legs and directs a stream of urine over the lady, soaking her. This makes a deep impression on her and she succumbs to his advances.

Shortly after the first encounter, she will offer herself to all and sundry, so long as they spray her first. She does not harm her partners with her quills. She raises her tail over her back and flattens her spines to provide a soft mattress for her lovers.

## POSSUMS

There are two distinct families of possum: New World 'possums and Australian possums. Note the apostrophe. It makes for confusion. Opossums have their own section in this book.

There are about 27 possum species in Australia belonging to the Phalangeridae family of marsupial mammals. They come in all sizes, from the 7gr 'little pygmy possum' up to the leopard-sized 'brushtail possum'.

The brushtail female gives birth to one offspring at a time which stays in mother's pouch until it gets too big by which time it is old enough to hitch a ride on her back until it decides to set up home for itself. Females mature at the age of one. Males wait until they are two. Common bushtails have an average life expectancy of 11 years.

Other possums include the honey possum, which has no claws and feeds on nectar. Then there are the gliders that have developed membranes to help them glide. They chatter a lot. There are all sorts of pygmy possums, some with long tails, some with none and some who do little else but sleep. Others include Ringtails and the Greater Gliders of the forests who are supposed to have a penchant for lemon scented gum.

The common brushtail possum is cultivated for its fur. It was introduced to New Zealand where it has no natural predators. It bred so successfully that it became officially outlawed as a pest. In that country alone there are estimated to be over 30,000,000 of them.

## PRAYING MANTISES

In laboratory conditions, females frequently bite off the heads of the males during mating. The male's thrusting automatically continues uninhibitedly, ensuring sperm delivery and increasing the chances of conceiving.

It is now in dispute whether this behaviour occurs in the wild. Mantises are extremely sensitive to light, and engaging in sex in laboratories, while being scrutinised through microscopes by scientists, may cause the female mantis to behave uncharacteristically.

Studies continue in the mantises' native environment in order to get a clearer picture of their mating behaviour. So far, it has been found that the male engages in an elaborate courtship dance to distract the female away from food and to concentrate her attention on sex. It seems unlikely that he would go to all this trouble if he thought he was going to get his head bitten off.

## PROTOZOA

A protozoa is a creature consisting of one cell. It reproduces by splitting into two. We should be respectful to it: the protozoa is our ultimate ancestor.

## PUFFINS

Due to a decline in the proliferation of sand-eels, some colonies of puffins are dying out in the UK. There is a concerted campaign to reverse this trend centering on the Farne Islands off Northumberland and at Skomer Island off Pembrokeshire. When their favoured food is not in short supply, puffins can collect up to 60 fish in their beaks at one time. They can be seen on shore between April and August.

# Q

## QUOLLS

(One cannot help thinking that along with kiwis, kangaroos and koalas, quolls should be spelt with a 'K'.) Quolls are carnivorous marsupials native to Australasia, first discovered in 1770 by Captain Cook. They have a superficial resemblance to polecats and weigh anything from 11oz (300gr) to 15lb (7kg). They are solitary animals and only meet for mating or for using the communal latrines. They have spotted coats and long bushy tails. Their breeding season occurs at the end of the winter.

They all come into heat simultaneously which leads to a frantic fight amongst both males and females desirous of the chance to propagate. The males are ruthless in this regard, dragging away as many females as they can get their claws into and rutting for as long as three hours at a time. This has been known to have repercussions on the males who exhaust themselves sometimes so thoroughly that they never recover.

Once the female has been impregnated, the folds on her stomach transform into a pouch that opens at the back. The pups are born after three weeks, sometimes as many as 18 to a litter, each no bigger than a grain of rice. The mother has only six teats in her newly formed pouch with the consequence that only six of the litter ever survive. All five species of quoll are endangered.

## RABBITS AND HARES

The gestation period for rabbits is from 30 to 35 days, and the kits are sexually mature at six months. They are prolific breeders. The communal burrows in which they live usually contain several breeding females, many of whom are pregnant or lactating, or both simultaneously. The average doe produces a litter of six kits.

One of the differences between rabbits and hares is seen in the birth of their kits. A baby hare is born with 20-20 vision and hair. A baby rabbit is born blind but bald. Another difference between them is that hares (and cottontail rabbits) make nests and live above ground whereas all other rabbits live in burrows.

The practice of coprophagy (the eating of one's own faeces) is, on the face of it, a disgusting rabbit habit. In fact, it is no worse than a cow regurgitating and chewing cud. The droppings of a rabbit are full of minerals and friendly bacteria and Vitamin B – all good things needed for a rabbit's well-being.

## RACCOONS AND COATIS

The raccoon has a black mask round his eyes that at first glance, makes him look like the Lone Ranger. He is an American mammal of the Procyonidae family (procyonid means a tree-climbing mammal) closely related to bears.

In the south of the country raccoons mate later than their New York cousins who get it together in February and March. They have special locations where they congregate to go through their courting rituals. Male raccoons go around scouting for females during the three to four days when conception is possible. Copulation can last for over an hour and is often repeated over several days with the same partner. The average gestation period is just over two months. A typical litter comprises two to five kits. They are suckled for four months before being weaned. Females will remain close to their mother. Males move away and form bachelor colonies. In the wild it is rare for a raccoon to live longer than three years but urban animals such as those adapted to life in the city of New York can survive until the age of 16.

## RATS

The gestation period for rats is three weeks. The female rat is sexually insatiable and she can produce 12 litters every year, each one consisting of 22 baby rats, and if the conditions are good, a rat's lifespan is five years, so that adds up to well over1000 rattlings during the life of one female rat. In the UK there are estimated to be 75,000,000 rats.

## RATTLESNAKES

There are 32 species of the highly venomous rattlesnake – all native to the US. Their fangs can leave painful memories. In North America, rattlesnake bites cause the largest number of snake injuries. If any creature comes across one of them, the snake gives due warning of imminent danger by vigorously shaking its tail producing a titular rattle.

When the mating season comes along, during the spring or the fall – depending on the species – the female exudes the necessary pheromones that males detect and follow by sticking out their tongues and using their *Vomeronasal* organ – the olfactory sense organ found in the mouth of many animals who react to pheromones with the flehmen response (*see Flehmen Response*).

## RED PANDAS

Not to be confused with the Panda (*see Panda*), the Red Panda is the size of a large domestic cat. In fact its scientific name translates as 'shining cat'. It is unique unto itself, belonging to the family Ailuridae of which all other members are extinct.

The fur of the Red Panda is reddish brown, his tail is shaggy and he has long white whiskers. He likes bamboo (there's a lot of it about in south-western China), but he is happy to tuck into small mammals, birds and eggs.

His wristbone has developed into a sort of 'false thumb' that enables him (like the panda) to climb headfirst down tree trunks. He is a solitary animal and does his foraging at night. Such behaviour is known as 'crepuscular'.

The mating season lasts for eight weeks from January to March. Both sexes indulge in any number of indiscriminate couplings during this time. Red Pandas whistle to communicate, and announce their presence by oozing musky secretions from their anal glands.

In anticipation of parturition, the female red panda will gather leaves and grass to prepare three or four nests, which are usually in hollow trees or concave rocks. After a gestation period of about four months, the female gives birth to blind and deaf cubs weighing on average just 4oz (120gr). The litter usually numbers four. The mother recognises them by smell and spends the first three months grooming and feeding them. She rotates the cubs from nest to nest in order to avoid predators but also to give herself time to keep the nests clean.

Once the mating season has finished, the males go off to continue their isolated existence for another year. The life-span of Red Pandas is between eight and 12 years. It is estimated that there are fewer than 3000 left in the wild. They are at the mercy of snow leopards, martens and the destruction of their bamboo habitat.

## REINDEER

Reindeer are chiefly famous for pulling Father Christmas's sleigh. It is often said that reindeer and caribou are the same animal, but there are subtle differences. The breeding season for reindeer starts in mid-August; for caribou they don't start until a month later. Reindeer are often pinto coloured whereas caribou never are.

Both sexes of reindeer grow antlers, although the males' are somewhat larger. Their favourite food is lichen, commonly known as 'reindeer moss'. In winter, their feet adapt so that the rims of their hooves are exposed to keep the animal from slipping on the ice. This is known as 'cratering'. It also enables the deer to cut through the snow to find the lichen they love to eat.

The males will fight each other for available females. An alpha male can mate with up to 20 females. This does not give him much time to munch moss and he loses a good deal of weight.

Gestation takes up to 230 days and mothers give birth to a single calf in May or June. They are weaned after a further eight weeks, but remain close to their mothers for protection from their two chief predators, golden eagles and wolverines. They are large enough to take care of themselves by the time the next rutting season begins. Young reindeer become sexually mature at two years old. Their life expectancy is about 18 years.

## REPTILES

Reptiles are cold blooded and belong to a classification of animal known as *Reptilia*. What they have in common is that they lay eggs (they are oviparous) and they are all covered with horny and bony skin.

The four known orders of reptiles are:

1) Crocodylia. This includes crocodiles, alligators, the caymans, and the gharials.
2) Rhynchocephalia. Specifically the tuatora – just two species. (Rhynchocephalia means 'beak-headed'.)
3) Squamata. Including lizards and snakes – 9000 species.
4) Testudines. Such as tortoises.

Reptiles have mating rituals. Some lizards change colour to signify their sexual readiness. Male turtles woo their ladies by bobbing heads and caressing the females face with his claws. Some reptiles have cloacae whereas others like the turtle have penises. Snakes and lizards have a pair of structures called 'the hemipenis'.

In most cases, male reptiles penetrate the cloacae of the females to ejaculate sperm into them. Embryos coalesce in the amniotic fluid and eventually eggs are laid covered with calcareous or leathery shells.

There are at least six types of lizard that are asexual and produce parthenogenetically. Being neither male nor female, no partner is needed to produce genetically identical clones of the parent. The number of eggs produced at one time varies dramatically. African tortoises achieve one or two at a time. Sea turtles produce 150. Upon hatching, all reptiles are fully developed.

## RHINOCEROSES

Mature rhinoceroses are solitary beasts. They tend to congregate at the end of the rainy season for the mating ritual. When in oestrus, the females mark dung piles. Males track them and scatter the dung to divert potential rivals from picking up the female's scent. Before mating, it is essential for rhinos to indulge in foreplay, which typically lasts for up to four hours. The males snort and spar with each other, sometimes running away like dogs before scurrying back, swinging their heads from side to side. The actual mating process can last up to 40 minutes, and the male may copulate three or four times a day over a week.

The gestation period lasts for up to 16 months and at birth, a calf can weigh 80 to 119lbs (35-50kls). The baby rhino is capable of walking after three days but weaning is not completed for another two years. The baby stays with its mother until she becomes pregnant again, which may be two or three years later.

The natural predators of calves are lions and hyenas. Females reach sexual maturity from 5 to 7 years old; males take a year longer. The life expectancy for a rhino in the wild is from 35 to 50 years.

According to statistics supplied by Rhinoceros International, there are currently about 5,000 black rhinoceroses and 20,400 white rhinoceroses left in Africa. These figures are falling rapidly. On average, two rhinos are being killed and poached for their horns every day. This slaughter is by no means humane. Once the horns have been cut out, the animals are left in agony to suffer a lingering death.

# S

## SALAMANDERS AND NEWTS

Salamanders are amphibians with four toes on their front legs and five toes on their back legs. They come in a variety of sizes, from the tiny (Thorius – half an inch long) to the huge (Andrias Davidianus – six feet long and weighing in at 5 stone).

In prehistoric times, salamanders were enormous. Salamanders that return to the water to breed are called newts. If ever they damage themselves by losing a limb or an organ, they can regenerate the missing part. Salamanders are the only known vertebrate to possess this ability. The process is subject to intense scientific scrutiny in the hope that there can be better understanding of growing and/or destroying rogue cells. The ultimate aim of such a study is to be able to control cancer cells.

Salamanders put on a courtship display at breeding time and they become markedly gregarious. The male deposits his spermatozoa sac, which is picked up by the female with her cloaca where the sperm is absorbed. The female can delay fertilisation until she is ready and this takes place internally.

She prefers calm, fresh water in which to lay her eggs. They develop into larvae that have tiny teeth and breathe through gills. This intermediate stage is of variable duration. Eventually, they lose the use of their gills, develop legs and begin their life on land. They use their sticky tongues to catch their food, which is wide-ranging, from earthworms to moths, from grasshoppers to spiders.

## SALMON AND TROUT

A hen salmon, heavily pregnant, will leap up rivers to spawn. Bouncing upstream on her stomach helps to release the eggs. Male (cock) salmon follow to the spawning pools where they vie with each other to deposit their milt (sperm) over the eggs. Then, if the bears and the anglers and other predators don't get them first, the exhausted males die. Some female Atlantic salmon survive spawning and return to the sea. Reports have been confirmed where the same salmon have returned to spawn two or three more times. These are rare events. Over 90 per cent of Atlantic salmon, and all Pacific salmon, die once they have achieved their reproductive purpose.

Scientists announced in *Current Biology* that salmon navigate across thousands of miles back to the river where they were born by correlating with the intensity of the Earth's geomagnetic field, which tends to drift over time.

Trout and salmon are so closely related that it is difficult to classify their individuality. Unlike most salmon, trout tend to spend much of their lives in fresh water, although sea trout migrate to the sea and return to their native rivers to spawn. Some rainbow trout, which are native to cold-water rivers of the Pacific coasts of North America and Asia, are also migratory, and these are generally known as steelhead. In 1989, DNA tests revealed that the rainbow trout is really a salmon. Further DNA tests discovered that the Atlantic salmon is really a trout.

## SAURIANS

Saurians were the first creatures to develop the penis and the vagina. Saurians include crocodiles, tortoises and lizards.

## SCORPIONS

Scorpions are related to spiders but have evolved to have a different kind of life. When in courting mood, the male scorpion gives the female of his choice a playful sting. Fortunately, scorpions are immune to their own venom.

He scratches a hollow in the earth into which he drops his sac of semen. She grabs one of his pincers with her claw and they arm-wrestle for a while, getting to know each other. Then she dances round in the fashion of a Scottish lady doing the Highland Fling. At last, she positions herself over the sperm sac. She takes possession and fertilisation follows. The female has a primitive womb and the gestation period of a scorpion can last for 10 months. Going into labour, the birthing process takes several days.

Eventually, she gives birth to live young – hundreds of baby scorpions. Their first instinct is for self-preservation. They waste no time before climbing onto their mother's back, seeking protection under the shadow of her stinger. Any scorpion baby who is slow in his feet is doomed. Nothing can protect the newborn offspring from their mother if she is feeling the pangs of hunger following her labour pains.

## SEA COWS (*SEE MANATEES AND DUGONGS*)

## SEAHORSES

The *Hippocampus*, or seahorse, has one of most bizarre sex lives. Unlike most female fish, the lady seahorse is the one wearing the flashy coloured scales. She possesses a genital papilla that looks like a nipple. To the untrained eye it is often mistaken for a penis. When mating, they face each other, belly to belly. She rams her papilla into her partner's stomach pouch wherein he stores his sperm. Then she releases her eggs like a soda-stream into his receptacle. He fertilises them and inside his pouch he exudes nutritious liquid in which the small-fry develop. The embryonic seahorse progeny live in his sex pouch and the lady seahorse swims away on the lookout for another male partner. Meanwhile, the babies develop in the father and their presence make him appear to be pregnant, which, in a sense, he is. After about two weeks, his sex-pouch flies open and thousands of baby seahorses are discharged into the water.

## SEALS AND SEA LIONS

The mating habits of seals, and their cousins the sea lions, leave a lot to be desired. If feminist groups existed in seal colonies, the population would rapidly die out. Male seals are often at least six times the size of the females. A male elephant seal gets boisterous during the sex act and quite often he can crush his partner to death.

A male seal may have as many as 50 female companions who are mercilessly beaten if they stray out of their master's territory. Sometimes, the males team up, all boys together, to share their territory, in which case the colonies develop into the thousands, controlled by 'beachmasters' consisting of half-a-dozen mafia-style males.

When mating, the females respond noisily and become the focus of attention for all lusty males in the area who rush to participate in the gang-bang with the result that up to two-thirds of the pup-seals are crushed to death in the mayhem.

Once the 3-week period of weaning is over, a cow elephant seal becomes sexually active again. Hungry, she enters the sea. The dominant bull and his acolytes watch her, knowing that she is still ripe for another sexual encounter. Together the males edge towards her, although it is always the beachmaster who is first served. He opens his jaws, grabs her roughly by the scruff of her neck and indulges himself until, satiated, he leaves her to the mercy of the other bulls.

## SHARKS

A male shark does not possess a penis but it uses pelvic fins to guide its gonopods and transfer sperm into the female shark's egg receptacle. Female sand tiger sharks are lucky to get out of the womb alive. Before they are born, the embryos attack and kill each other.

## SHEEP

Sheep are cattle. If they hadn't been domesticated and farmed they would probably be extinct by now. It is estimated that there are well over a billion sheep in the world – one-sixth of the human population. The gestation period for sheep is 144 to 152 days.

It is outside the scope of this book to look at the mating habits of livestock since farmed animals are bred in artificial conditions. Suffice to say domesticated animals are subject to experiment. In 1984 (a significant year, you might think) the Institute of Animal Physiology in Cambridge, UK, successfully combined sheep embryos with goat embryos. The resultant animal is called a chimera, and this particular chimeric animal was given a name; it was called a geep. The parts that grew from a goat embryo were hairy, and those that grew from a sheep embryo were woolly. As to what point this experiment was making is anybody's guess.

## SHREWS

The life expectancy of shrews, which are common in England, is about 14 months. They are solitary animals except when seeking a mate. The common shrew's breeding season peaks in mid-summer. The gestation period is typically 25 days and the female will then give birth to up to seven babies. It is common to see young shrews follow their mother, caravan-style, each baby carrying in its mouth the tail of the sibling in front.

Shrews are active day and night and burn off a lot of energy and fat. To maintain their weight and lifestyle, they have to eat every two or three hours. Though nearly blind, their hearing is exceptional and this enables them to seek out insects, worms, slugs and even voles.

# SKINK

Skink are a type of lizard belonging to the *Scincidae* family. They are secretive little fellows and most of them stay out of sight in their burrows. A few have adapted to living in trees. There are at least 1200 species of skink, making this the largest family of lizards after geckos (Gekkonidae). Skink have tiny limbs and hardly any necks. They have a sort of transparent eye-shield, which protects them as they burrow, whilst at the same time allowing them to see where they are going. They have the ability to shed their tails and regenerate them. Some skink return to the scene where they lost their tails and then eat them, restoring some of their lost energy.

During the breeding season when testosterone levels rise, the heads of the males increase in size and turn a reddish colour. In the roof of their mouths they posses what is known as the Jacobson organ that is highly sensitive to chemical signals sent out by the opposite sex. The males become aggressive with each other and, triggered by the pheromones, pursue the females. About half of all skink are ovoviviparous, meaning they hatch their eggs internally and give birth to live offspring. Some skink give birth to live young *and* lay eggs in alternate breeding seasons.

# SKUNKS

Skunks are sometimes called polecats. They do look like small cuddly creatures, but the word skunk seems a more appropriate word for them than cat. Their name probably derives from an Algonquian dialect word, seganku, which roughly translated means urinating fox.

Skunks mate in early spring and there is no question of

monogamy. First come, first served, as the expression goes. Round about May, the female will dig a burrow, called a den and after a gestation period of 66 days, she gives birth to her kits, sometimes as many as seven. Their eyes open after three weeks and stay on the breast altogether for about three months. They don't leave the den for the first year.

They have two scent glands, situated on either side of their anus, and these are used as defensive weapons. The scent is a mixture of sulphur, industrial gas and garlic. They tend to employ this only when they are extremely frightened. In normal circumstances – in a dispute involving love rivalry, for example – they prefer to fight with tooth and claw. They posses less than 15cc of the noxious gas in their bodies at any given time and they conserve it whenever possible, as it takes a couple of weeks to accumulate another supply.

## SLOTHS

Sloths are vegetarian mammals and come in two shoe sizes: two-toed and three-toed. They live in trees in South America and are cousins of anteaters. Many species of sloth have died out, and that may be a good thing, as at one time they were, apparently, the size of elephants.

Sloths spend most of their time hanging upside down. Over the years this has caused their hair to grow in the opposite direction to most mammals, giving them a fringe around their faces rather similar to the early Beatles.

The female sloth reaches sexual maturity at three, the male a year later. There is no doubt left in anybody's mind when a female sloth comes into oestrus, because she starts screaming. Some of the males slink away at this point, but one or two might summon up the energy to see what her problem is.

Hanging upside down, he mounts her and, taking his time, gets into the business of copulation. He may doze off and then the lady, in her impatience, turns round to face him, whether to reprimand him or to get more comfortable is difficult to define. They resume intercourse, this time face-to-face but it may take the male an hour or more to come to the point.

## SLUGS AND SNAILS

Snails are hermaphrodites, meaning they have both male and female sexual organs, but they do not self-fertilise. Their genitals are situated in a place that turns out to be convenient for snails – just behind their eye-stalks.

Before a couple of snails mate, they shoot 'love darts' at each other. It used to be thought that these sharp barbs contained something nutritional, but they are actually made of calcium. A snail lays over half a million eggs at a time. Being hermaphrodites, they can have sex with themselves. Indeed, they take the opportunity to do this as often as they can get their breath back. To the Greeks, a snail was a gastropod, meaning 'stomach-foot'. Roman snails, on a midnight date, will stick together, foot-to-foot, and throb a lot.

They possess enormous penises, or *gypsobalum* as they are known to we common folk. They proceed to insert their gypsobalums into each other's vaginas enabling them to exchange small packets of sperm (spermatophores). After their union, they fall apart and take a considerable time to recover their composure. Their penises are commonly one-fifth the length of a snail's entire foot. Penis lengths change with the annual reproductive cycle.

The banana slug is eight inches long and is blessed with an eight-inch penis, but the blessing proves to be a curse in disguise. To find a female slug big enough to accommodate such a huge organ takes the male slug on a virtually permanent quest to find a large lady. When he comes across a likely mate he is wrong to assume that his mission is accomplished. The new partner will boggle at the vast penis, balk at the issue and then start to gnaw his gypsobalum down to a manageable size. Thus it is understood that the male banana slug doesn't have sex very often.

## SNAKES

Adders have declined in numbers by half since the 1960s. In the UK it is estimated that there are fewer than 1000 separate populations surviving, with the greatest density in Dorset, the New Forest, Surrey, and Greenham Common, Berkshire. There are no snakes in Ireland.

Ordinarily, a male snake rubs himself up against a female, running his tongue up and down her back, and curling his body around hers before setting off a ripple of muscle contractions that melt her heart.

In North America, garter snakes hibernate underground until the spring when they emerge blinking into the unaccustomed light. Lady garter snakes emit a burst of pheromones to make her presence known to any male garter snakes that may be awakening with the joys of spring. The males go wild with excitement and wriggle out of their holes, heading for the female as fast as their bellies can carry them. Simultaneously, thousands of garter snakes get the urge. They twist and turn trying to reach her cloaca with their double-headed penises that are normally concealed by their anus. One of these penises is slightly bulkier than the other. Hundreds of them join in and writhe about in what is termed 'a mating ball'. Eventually, one of the males gets lucky and the losers slink off sulkily.

There are occasions when one of the losers plays a sneaky game on the others. He will mimic the emission of female pheromones, causing the males to think he is of the feminine gender. So they jump on him. But he is not homosexual. By the time they have discovered their mistake, they have worn themselves out sufficiently for the trickster to go after a true lady without any competition.

## SPERMATHECA

The *New Shorter Oxford English Dictionary* defines spermatheca as: 'A receptacle in a female or hermaphrodite animal in which sperm is stored.'

## SPERMATOPHORE

The *New Shorter Oxford English Dictionary* gives the following definition: 'A protein capsule containing a mass of spermatozoa, transferred during mating in various insects and other invertebrates.'

## SPIDERS

The female black widow spider found in the US is notoriously dangerous. Her black, bulbous body has red or yellow marks shaped like an hourglass under the abdomen. Her legs are long and she is, on average, 30 times bigger than the male black widow spider. She is a solitary creature except when that time of year comes round to indulge in the deadly mating ritual.

When consummation is imminent, the male black widow approaches his mate tentatively, not without reason, particularly if he has been watching what became of the other gentlemen who once belonged to his club.

She sits in the web watching, waiting for him. As he nears her, he performs a courting ritual that involves knee-bending and tapping his legs. It is possible that humans misinterpret this. We may be witnessing the male spider's fear of what is to come, causing his knees to knock together, though it is unlikely.

Actually, male spiders do not have a penis. They secrete sperm into a web specially spun to accommodate it. This is then sucked up into his *pedipalps* – a specially adapted leg with a holder for his bunch of sperm.

The female stays perfectly still while the little fellow crawls onto her back and begins the sperm transferral process. He inserts his pedipalps into her corresponding opening, locks it in securely and the sperm is injected into her as if by a hypodermic syringe.

Unfortunately, her genital opening has a tight grip on things and sometimes the husband's penis may break off in her. Whether or not this occurs, the male will make a quick tactical retreat on completion of the ritual. Sometimes he gets clean away. At other times, the female widow spider decides it is time for a snack and she will catch him, dissolve him and drink in his juices.

She stores his sperm in her ovulatory sac and fertilises her eggs, up to 1000 of them. Her sac is a cocoon of woven silk about half-an-inch in diameter. As the eggs mature, the colour of the sac changes from white to brown. It can take many months for the eggs to hatch and when they do, the female widow spider will regard them as tasty delicacies. She eats them, leaving behind perhaps a dozen survivors.

A female black widow can mate up to two dozen times a day although she only bothers to eat three or four of her husbands. Certain female spiders (and Praying Mantises) eat their male lovers after copulation. A Black Widow Spider can get through 20 husbands a day: talk about being hungry for sex.

The male crab spider does not have to run for his life after sex. He embraces his beloved with all eight of his legs and the two continue to have a warm and fruitful relationship.

## SPONGES

*Romantic sponges, they say, do it,*
*Oysters, down in oyster bay, do it...*
(LYRICS BY COLE PORTER)

One of the oldest life forms is the sponge. It is a hermaphrodite. At different stages of its life cycle it produces both sperm and egg. So far as is known, it does not fertilise itself. Perhaps this is a precaution against in-breeding. I certainly wouldn't want to see my sponge mating with itself. It might get soap in its eyes.

## SQUIRRELS AND CHIPMUNKS

Britain's native Red Squirrel population has been decimated in recent years. There are fewer than 150,000 remaining. The decline started in 1876 when the grey squirrel was introduced from America. There are now more than 3,000,000 grey squirrels. They carry the squirrel-pox virus and are more aggressive in the competition for food. The gestation period for squirrels is 44 days.

Chipmunks are squirrel-like rodents found mostly in North America. In the early days of colonisation they were called chip-squirrels. They have two breeding seasons: spring and early autumn, although they generally conceive only once a year. They produce litters of four to five and the young chipmunks do not venture out of the burrow until six or seven weeks old.

They construct elaborate burrows as long as four metres, with many concealed entrances and escape hatches. They have separate chambers with specific functions. There is one for refuse, another kept as a latrine and another – well-stocked with food – is their larder. Sometimes they have to dig in for a long winter. Their living quarters are kept immaculately clean. Even so, the females are left alone to bring up the kids.

## STARFISH AND SEA-URCHINS

Sea urchins come from the same family as starfish and sea cucumbers. They are called *echinoderms* (spiny skins) and this means those creatures that have the outward appearance of being radially symmetrical. In fact, they all look so similar that it is difficult, if not impossible, for a human to spot the difference between a male and a female.

Both sexes have five gonads attached to their legs that are on the side of their mouths. If it is a male, he will emit sperm from these gonads. If a female, eggs, two and a half million eggs at a time. Her pheromones attract the males who deposit their sperm over the eggs. In any given area, sea urchins will all spontaneously spawn at once. It is believed that this is caused by a number of conditions coming together: temperature, plankton availability and those all-important pheromones.

During the mass spawning, once a sperm reaches an egg, fertilisation takes place. In the early stages, they look like the plankton they feed on. Gradually, they metamorphose into starfish. They congregate in huge numbers and sweep across the seabed as one, consuming everything in their path, from mussels to oysters. It is estimated that up to 90 per cent of the millions of eggs don't make it. The gonads of sea urchins are considered a great delicacy by the Japanese who consume tons of them every year.

## STICK INSECTS

Stick insects are also called walking sticks and stick-bugs. They belong to an order of insects known as Phasmatodea. This derives from an Ancient Greek word meaning phantom, because they can disguise themselves to look identical to leaves or sticks or even other insects.

Some types of stick insect are parthenogenic – they don't need a mate to reproduce. But some do, and a female can lay from 100 to 1200 eggs depending on the species. She will deposit them on a host plant so they have something to feed on when they hatch. If they are creatures born without fertilisation they will all be female. Otherwise, there is the normal mixture of the sexes.

Their gift for disguise is present even at the larval stage. Sometimes the eggs of stick insects have a fatty substance attached to them, which ants find so tasty they drag the eggs back to their nest to chew the fat there. When the eggs hatch, a tiny stick insect nymph emerges disguised as the nymph of an ant.

Needless to say, the ants believe he is one of the family and leave him to his own devices. As soon as their backs are turned, the tiny stick insect scarpers and gets out of the nest before they discover he is an interloper. Next, he climbs up a suitable plant on which he can nibble and very soon he changes shape and manages to fool all-comers that he is a leaf or a twig of the host on which he is actually feeding.

## SWANS

Geese and swans mate for life – staying together for 50 years or longer. A widowed goose or a drake widower will sink into a deep depression, continually searching for the lost partner. The widow ganders may well set up shop together in a largely platonic relationship. Sometimes a goose will come along and fall in love with one of the odd couple; this can result in a *ménage-a-trois*.

## TAPIRS

Tapirs look similar to pigs, though their closest cousins are horses and rhinoceroses. They have poor eyesight and spend a great deal of time underwater, sometimes taking walks upon the riverbed looking for fish. The nose, or proboscis, of a tapir is capable of moving in any direction, allowing the animal to take full advantage of its remarkable sense of smell. It is often seen displaying the 'flehmen response', particularly in the mating season when the males are sniffing around searching for the scent of a female in oestrus.

They are solitary animals and, like rhinos, only congregate to mate. Male tapirs reach sexual maturity at 4, with the females getting there a year earlier. They sometimes copulate in water, and intercourse is repeated several times during the period of oestrus. The penetrative act lasts a quarter of an hour.

Proportionate to their body size, male tapirs have exceptionally long penises. The female typically produces a single baby tapir once every two years, the offspring sporting a striped-and-spotted coat for camouflage. The gestation period is 13 months. The natural lifespan of tapirs is about 27 years. Unfortunately, they are another endangered species.

## TENRECS

Tenrecs, mammals which resemble shrews or hedgehogs, are found mainly in Madagascar. Their favourite diet is insects. Tailless and spiny, they manage to breed well and the mother can produce a litter of 32 tiny tenrecs.

## TERMITES

(*To distinguish termites from ants, see 'Ants'.*) Termites have evolved from cockroaches and there genus is *blattodea*. Termites live in colonies containing millions. At the apex of termites' social hierarchy are the king and queen who mate for life. Depending on the species, the queen can lay more than 80,000 eggs per day.

A pregnant queen expands as her ovaries swell with eggs. Before laying, she sometimes develops to be 300 times her original size. A female termite can produce over 50,000,000 offspring in a lifetime. It is estimated that 4 per cent of the methane produced on earth comes from termites.

At the bottom of the social heap are the workers – quite blind – who eat wood and regurgitate the indigestible cellulose as negotiable food for their peer group to survive.

## TERRAPINS

Terrapin is an Algonquin word meaning turtle. In America terrapin refers to the species who live in brackish water – the diamondback terrapin, so called because of the patterns on the backs of their shells. In the UK, terrapin includes those turtles that live in fresh water. Large marine terrapins engage in sexual intercourse whilst swimming, and can perform both acts simultaneously, for several days.

Being reptiles, fertilisation in female terrapins occurs internally. The mating season begins towards the end of May and the females mate with multiple males, resulting in clutches of eggs with more than one father. As in the crocodile, the determination of the offspring's sex is ruled by the exterior temperature. The female typically lays three clutches of eggs per year. Nests are built in sand dunes near the ocean. Once laid and covered, the eggs are left to hatch by themselves and the mothers return to the water. It takes two to three months for the eggs to hatch. The hatchlings tend to remain in their nesting area to feed before venturing to water once they have started to mature.

## TIGERS

The tiger is the largest of the cat species; the next size down is the lion. A tiger is immediately recognisable because of its vertical black stripes, which are unique to each tiger and not only patterned in the hair; the skin beneath is also striped identically. The Bengal tiger is the national symbol of both India and Bangladesh.

Hybridisation between a male lion and a tigress is called a liger; that between a male tiger and a lioness is called a tigon.

Such experimentations are discouraged in most zoos today but the practice is popular in China.

In the wild, tigers are solitary animals. Unlike most cats (with the exception of jaguars with which they share this facility) they love to bathe and are good swimmers. Unlike lions, who eat selfishly, both male and female tigers are content to share their kills amicably. Similarly, although territorial, males and females are more tolerant of younger generations of their own sex sharing part of their territory.

The breeding season occurs between November and April. A female comes into oestrus for only three to five days and she takes full advantage of these periods by mating frequently and noisily. The mother-to-be searches out a birthing site in a sheltered spot in a rocky crevice or a cave. The average gestation period is 105 days and the litter is typically three.

The cubs are born blind and helpless. Fifty per cent of them do not survive the first two years, victim to predators, starvation, freezing and poachers. They open their eyes within two weeks, and stay in their mother's den until they are weaned after about six months. During this time, they are taught how to hunt and by the time they are 18 months old, they start to attempt hunting for themselves. Females reach sexual maturity at about 4; males take a year longer.

Tigers can live to the age of 25 – all 3,200 of them, for there are only that number left in the wild. In the US, there may be the same number alive in zoos and private parks, but these beautiful creatures need all the protection they can get.

## TOADS

Toads have the ability to change from being male to female. It takes time, but turns out to be useful in populations where lady toads are scarce.

The difference between toads and frogs is mainly one of appearance. A toad has warty skin. A frog has smooth skin. A toad waddles. A frog hops. One of the toad's favourite snacks is the moist woodlouse.

Toads produce up to 7000 eggs per laying. There is a male toad in Europe that puts his fist into a lady toad's cloaca and pulls out her string of eggs. These he wraps around his hind legs. He visits other lady friends and does the same with them, always wrapping the eggs round his legs until he can hardly move. He waddles into shallow water until such time as the tadpoles are independent and they drop off him like so many pearls.

## TORTOISES AND TURTLES

Tortoises are cold-blooded herbivores. The standard for telling the difference between a turtle and a tortoise is that a turtle has flippers while a tortoise has feet. Even so, the definitions vary slightly in different countries. In the UK, tortoises are regarded as land animals that cannot swim. In Australia tortoises are seen as semi-aquatic.

They reach sexual maturity between 20 and 30, barely in adolescence for a tortoise. The Maine tortoise takes his time and can enjoy a sexual dalliance for several days. Mating is a cumbersome affair that happens, not often but sometimes, on hot summer days. They have excellent night vision but in the daytime their eyesight is so rotten they depend greatly on pheromones transmitting the correct hormonal signals. Head-bobbing takes place, indicating some sort of willingness to get on with it, but since neither the male nor the female see so well, this may be a futile gesture. The clash of a 'cloacal kiss' takes such a lot of effort it is an experience that elderly tortoises don't particularly want to repeat in a hurry.

Female tortoises dig burrows in the sand and lay their eggs in them at night – up to 30 at a time. The mother covers her clutch, as best she can, with sand and mulch and dying vegetation. The eggs are then left to get on with it and hatch by themselves, a process that can take anything from two to four months depending on the climate. When the self-incubation is complete, the hatchling will have grown an 'egg-tooth' which it uses like a tiny pick-axe to force its way out from inside the shell. The baby tortoise digs its way up to the surface though there is no knowing how long this can take – it could be hours but it may be days. Fortunately, it has emerged from the egg with an embryonic sac of albumen that provides the hatchling with enough nutrition to keep going without proper food for a few days.

It used to be said that the number of concentric rings that could be counted on the carapace would give the age of the creature, like counting the rings on a tree. Subsequently, this method has proved to be unreliable. However, it has been authenticated that some tortoises can live to over 150. In 1777, Captain Cook made a gift of a tortoise to the Tongan royal family. This old fellow kept going until 19 May 1965, by which time it was estimated to be at least 188. There are claims that a tortoise called Hanako who died on 17 July 1977 was 226.

## TOUCANS

Toucans are South American birds memorable for their blue eyes and enormous multi-coloured beaks – in the case of the common toucan it is a vivid orange-yellow. In some species, the bill weighs half of the total body weight of the bird.

The big toucans that are in the forefront of public perception are the Toco toucan and the Keel Bill. Toucans vary in size from 7ins up to 2ft. The blue we think we see in their eyes is actually a ring of blue skin surrounded by another ring of orange skin.

When a toucan sleeps he employs a joint at the base of his spine that enables him to flip his tail forward up and over his back to cover his neck. Then he tucks his head sideways and ends up disguising himself as a ball of feathers.

They are not good flyers and prefer to hop from tree to tree where they nest aloft in hollowed out nests. They get round to mating once a year. When they are about to mate the birds start to purr, the male regurgitates pieces of fruit as offerings to his partner and once she has accepted the love tokens, the collision of cloacae will shortly occur.

Three or four days after conception the female will lay an average of three or four white, glossy eggs. Clutch-sitting duties are shared equally between the parents, and the eggs take 17 to 18 days to hatch. The chicks emerge completely naked without any down. The parents are territorial and aggressively protective of their chicks.

Toucans reach sexual maturity at about three, although Toucanets and Aracaris – the smallest of this type of bird – start breeding earlier. The lifespan of toucans is about 24 years. Toucans used to be common and cheaply traded as pets and cage birds. Today, some species are endangered and are on the list of CITES (the Convention on International Trade in Endangered Species of Wild Fauna and Flora) which is an international agreement between governments. Its aim is to ensure that international trade in specimens of wild animals and plants does not threaten their survival.

## TUATARA

The tuatura are unique reptiles found in the wild, only in New Zealand. Tuatura is taken from the Maori language meaning 'peaks on the back'. They are direct descendants of dinosaurs, although they are only 30 inches long and weigh less than 3lb. As well as the spiny back, they have a third eye (called the parietal eye) the purpose of which is not certain. Some ethnologists conjecture that the third eye may be able to detect polarised light in cloudy weather thereby assisting navigation. Tuatara have no ears and yet they can hear. When threatened, they can lose their tails, but these will regenerate in time.

A second species of tuatara is found on Brother Island, a tiny island in the Cook Strait. This species differs from its cousins in colouring, being clad in mottled brown and yellow skin as opposed to the others' greenish orange. They all have transverse cloacal slits, meaning that these posterior openings are horizontal.

Tuaturas live for upwards of 200 years so they are in no great hurry to mate. In fact a male might not get the urge to woo until he is about 20. Then, in the summer – it has to be hot – the male will stiffen the crests on his back and the colour of his skin will darken. When he has sighted a likely mate, he walks round her slowly as if on tiptoe to appear butch and big. If the female likes what she sees, she will bow down and allow the male to lift her tail aside. The mating process is similar to that of birds. He mounts her and they press their cloacae together. Sperm passes from his body into hers and, with luck, the gestation process will begin. When successful, this can take up to 15 months. For this reason the lady tuatura only cares to mate every four years. When the eggs hatch in her burrow, another couple of years saunter by before the hatchlings desert the nest. Tuatara live long and leisurely lives.

## TURKEYS

Sometimes a turkey can fall in love with a peacock. It happened in 2012 at the Hopetown Estate in Linlithgow and resulted in the turkey being spared execution for Christmas.

## VOLES

The water vole is Britain's fastest declining mammal, mainly due to the introduction of the American mink. In 25 years the population of water voles has dropped from 10,000,000 to 900,000.

## VULTURES

There are two distinct types of vulture, the Old World vulture and the New World vulture. Extraordinarily enough, they are not related.

The American bird answers to several names: turkey vulture, turkey buzzard, John Crow or carrion cow. It roosts in large communes and nests in caves, though it only uses these in the breeding season. When the mating season comes around, which varies depending on whereabouts in the Americas they happen to be, turkey vultures perform their own variation of a lek where the males parade around showing off to the females.

They gather in a circle and do a sort of square dance and then a turkey trot with their wings spread out. A male will take flight and give an aerial display and if he is lucky a female will fly up to join him. At this point he knows he only has to play his cards right and sex is in the bag.

Typically, eggs are laid in a protected place such as the ledge of a cliff or inside a hollow tree. They don't bother with nests. These are new-age birds. As a rule, the hens lay two eggs on a bare surface – pretty eggs too, with lavender spots over a cream shell. The cock and the hen share the responsibilities of incubating the clutch, which takes just over a month. When the hatchlings break out of the shell, they are helpless and the parents feed them with regurgitated food for another couple of months. They are protective of their brood and can be aggressive if they think they are in danger. After three more months, the chicks are fully fledged but the family stays together as a unit until late autumn.

The culture of the Old World vulture seems similar. The European and African birds are also scavengers that feed off carrion. They tear at the carcasses of dead animals and this causes blood to splatter onto their heads. Hence, they have developed featherless, bald, red skulls so you can't tell if they are covered in blood or not.

# W

## WALRUSES

Like martens and dogs, walruses have bones in their penises that maintain an erection of at least two feet.

The females tend to imitate Mae West when courting. They lounge on the ice, leaning on a flipper and fluttering their eyelids as if to say, 'Come up and see me sometime.' Meanwhile, swimming in the surf like a pack of hungry wolves, the male walruses eye her up and down, splash about, make a rude trumpet calls and finally demonstrate their prowess by biting each other. Wooed like this, the ladies slip into the sea one by one and cavort with the escort of their choice. The paired couple take each other into deeper water where their act of union is accomplished.

The lady walrus is not promiscuous and once sexual congress is complete, she returns to her ice shelf and contemplates the spatter of tiny flippers.

## WASPS

There is a form of parasitic wasp which dispenses with the male sex altogether. The females lay eggs that are self-fertilised and therefore produce only female wasps.

The female fig wasp (*Pleistodontes froggatti*) lays her eggs inside the fruit of fig trees, where the larvae can develop and thrive. In return, the wasps pollinate the figs. However, if the wasp lays her eggs and doesn't fulfil her part of the bargain, the tree will wither the fig that contains her larvae and the fig will drop off and the eggs will die.

The sole function of the male fig wasp is to inseminate the developing female pupae within the fig before he laboriously bores a way out to the surface of the fruit. The females then trample all over him and leave him to die while they fly off to find another tree with figs. They lay their fertilised eggs, and the process starts all over again. It is said that this cycle has been going on for about 90,000,000 years.

Tinnid wasps are timid. The males have wings – the females don't. The males climb over the females, clasp them to their bodies, lift them and fly into the air with them. Then they mate with them in mid-air. It's the wasp's equivalent of the mile-high club.

## WHALES

Generally, whales mate face-to-face. They either do it laying side-by-side on the seabed or, vertically, standing on their tails with their heads above the water.

The blue whale is the largest animal on earth, and possibly the largest animal that has ever lived. It eats over 2 tons of food per day. A blue whale can weigh up to 175 tons and its penis can be as long as 7ft. It is calculated that there may be fewer than 10,000 blue whales left in the world.

In spring, they migrate to warmer climes to mate. Some marine biologists suspect the melodic noises that whales emit when they are in season are love songs. The sounds produced by whales underwater can be heard hundreds of miles away.

Little is known for certain about their mating habits. It is believed that the female southern right whale will mate with up to seven males who wait patiently in line for their turn.

Females give birth to a single calf approximately every three years, the gestation period having been over a year. Calves are born near the surface of the water. At parturition, these 3-ton babies are born tail first, and one of the first things the calf will do is poke its head out of the water and take a deep breath. They remain close to their mother for another seven or eight months, drinking as much as 100 gallons of milk every day. Their weight gain is about 200lb every 24 hours. No other animal has a faster rate of growth. At the same time, the female blue whale can lose 50 tons in weight while feeding her offspring. When the calves have attained a weight of around 23 tons, they stop being dependent on their mother's milk, although they keep in close proximity for another year or two.

The calves of an orca whale are at least 8ft in length at birth and they too are delivered tail first. Female orcas give birth every 10 years on average. There have been at least a dozen documented cases of hybrid whales, that is a cross between blue whales and fin whales. It is believed that their life span is about 100 years.

## WOLVES

Wolves are the ancestors of today's domestic dogs. The wolf, also known as the grey wolf, was first tamed about 16,000 years ago in China, just south of the Yangtze River.

Wild wolves are big – 6ft to 7ft from snout to tail. There are lone wolves but mostly they prefer to live in packs of about a dozen individuals (two adults, six juveniles and four yearlings). They howl to communicate, and they scent-mark their territory boundaries with urine specimens every 240 metres or so. They are carnivorous and have acquired a bad reputation for eating sheep.

In the wild, male wolves start breeding at the age of two. Oestrus occurs for females in late winter and lasts less than a month. She is capable of producing one litter per year.

Once wolves are paired, they stay together for life. Whenever the female is receptive, she raises her tail to expose her ripening vulva. The act of mating can be prolonged to 30 minutes, as the male's penis expands during intercourse causing what is known as a 'copulatory tie'. The same thing happens with domestic dogs, but wolves free themselves more easily. The male ejaculates several times and will copulate as often as he can during the limited time at his disposal during her period of oestrus.

In the spring, the bitch wolf gives birth to five or six blind, deaf pups. They open their eyes after about 10 days, and venture outside the den after three weeks. Their mother remains in the den to suckle and clean her pups, leaving the fetching of food and guard duty to the father. Pups put on weight quickly – increasing their weight more than 30 times in the first four months. By the autumn season the young wolves are strong enough to accompany their parents on hunting expeditions.

## WOODPECKERS

The pecking of a woodpecker is not just to dig a hole to find insects and grubs as was once believed. It is their equivalent of beating jungle drums – a way to communicate and an attempt to attract another pecker with whom to mate. It also enables them to get at the tree sap, a nourishing snack for a bird.

Once they have chosen a mate, they remain monogamous and excavate a cavity together by digging into a tree. When they have finished building this nest, it is neatly lined with wood chips in preparation for the two to five eggs. The male incubates at nights and it take 12 days for the eggs to hatch. The nestlings are fully fledged after four weeks.

## WORMS (ANNELIDS)

It's taken quite a few million years for the human being to evolve, but at some point in our ancestral heritage we resembled the prehistoric *annelid* – a worm. It was the first animal to develop an alimentary tract with openings at the front and at the rear, and that's the reason we have mouths and bottoms.

There are more than 22,000 species of worm, from rag worms to leeches. It is estimated that at least a million earthworms occupy every acre of land. Some types of worm – such as the *Aulophorus furcatus* – breed asexually. Bits of the parent drop off and these buds, as they are generally called, regenerate themselves and grow into replicas of their parent.

Others enjoy the privacy of their own asexuality during the spring but by autumn they get the urge to merge with a partner for some serious intertwining. Worms are under continuous scientific scrutiny but as yet what they get up to when nobody is watching cannot be described with any certainty. Worms can be a bit stand-offish, a characteristic passed down to their descendants.

Some of them are hermaphrodites, which means they can impregnate themselves. Some types start off as males and change into females at a later stage. There are a number of others that are of two separate sexes. These will release sperm and ova into the water and a normal 'fishy' fertilisation can take place. The resulting larvae turn into plankton and later metamorphose back into regular adult worms.

For flatworms, sex is more like war than love. As with all sea slugs, flatworms are hermaphrodites (they have both male and female sexual organs). In this case, the male organ turns out to be a two-pronged dagger-like penis with which he hunts as well as attempting to mate. Two flatworms, wishing to consummate their relationship, have to decide who is going to be mother by fighting, gladiator style, with their sharp penises. The 'loser' (or possibly the 'winner') is the one who gets stabbed first. 'He' is now a 'she' and absorbs the victor's sperm through the wound in her skin. Pregnant at last, she scoots off to prepare for the burden of motherhood.

Leeches are more sophisticated. They have well-defined gonads and copulate to achieve reproduction. Not much has changed over the millennia.

Earthworms also have the genitalia of both sexes. When they copulate, each impregnates the other: two offspring for the price of one. Earthworms have sacs called *spermathecae* where they store the sperm of their partner until such time as the sperm can be added to the eggs in the *clitellum*.

The clitellum on an earthworm can be seen as a raised

band encircling the body. The word derives from the Latin for saddlebag. This band assembles sperm and eggs together where they are cocooned and shaken like a cocktail mixer to become fertilised. The resulting wormlings hatch into miniature adults.

There is an eelworm that only lives in bumblebees. After mating, she burrows into the queen bee. Her vagina expands exponentially, absorbing the entire genital tract. Eventually, the body shrivels, leaving the worm in possession of nothing but an enlarged vagina in which her eggs develop as in a nest.

A certain genus of marine worm is pedantically romantic: they make love *only* when there is a full moon.

The roundworm goes by the scientific name of *Caenorhabditis elegans*. It is only in the last 40 years that this little creature has been studied in depth. It is a transparent nematode less than one millimetre in length. There are two types: hermaphrodites and males, but the male roundworm is something of a rarity existing in a ratio of about 1000:1. Males have a single-lobed gonad (*vas deferens*) and a specialised tail for mating purposes. Hermaphrodites take care of themselves with two ovaries, two oviducts, a spermsack and a uterus. An hermaphrodite lays about 300 eggs when self-fertilised but over 1000 if one of the rare males she may encounter has had conjugal relations with her/ him. When the eggs are hatched, the juvenile worms go through a larval stage. If there is no food about, the larvae can go into a dormant state for a considerable length of time in which they do not age. Studies are being made to discover if this extraordinary arrestment of the ageing process can be of significance to humans.

The female starworm, shaped like a gherkin, is the giant of her species. The male star worms are so small they live inside her vagina, living off their hostess's juices, and fertilising eggs as they come along.

A tapeworm lives for over 40 years and never stops mating. It can spawn a million eggs every day. Survival rates are unbelievably low. The eggs must leave the host and afterwards re-enter a new host – such a high-risk strategy that only one in a billion ever makes it. However, during the lifetime of an adult tapeworm, she can lay seven thousand million eggs.

When she gets the urge for lovemaking, the female threadworm will poke both her bottom and her vagina out of the surface of the vegetable upon which she happens to be feasting. The male threadworm will wriggle around the vegetable's skin until he comes across the object of his desire. He makes love there and then. He doesn't even ask her name.

Living on islands in the west Pacific is a foot-long worm called the palolo. It burrows deep into coral reefs eating the polyps. To breed, this worm backs out of its tunnel exposing its rear end, which snaps off. This back segment has a life of its own and makes its independent way up to the surface of the sea where it bursts like a bud distributing pollen. However, these sex cells need to connect to cells of the opposite gender in order to fertilise. This is the tricky bit.

All palolo worms must release their sex cells at exactly the same moment in order to stand any chance of reproducing. In some still unexplained way they do manage to pull off this trick of mingling simultaneously.

Twice a year, their timing is absolutely precise. Their emergence can be marked on the calendar in advance for the rest of time. It is always at sunrise on the first three days of the moon's third quarter in October; and again, in November, at exactly the same phase of the moon. Fishermen of the local islands do, in fact, mark their diaries and are ready with their nets, as are the worms predators – fish. A frenzied threshing takes place as countless millions of the worms' sex organs fill the sea and float towards the surface. This phenomenon takes place right across the Pacific, as, nearly a thousand miles apart, the worms surface simultaneously.

## ZEBRAS

Wild zebras were once common all over Africa but now they are only found in the south. There are three main species of zebras, which can all interbreed: they are the plains zebra (*Equus quagga*), Grevy's zebra (*Equus grevyi*) and mountain zebra (*Equus zebra*). Zebra breeding behaviour is very much like feral horses and feral donkeys.

Mares come into heat during the breeding season between January and March, but will only become pregnant when they are at their most fertile. A dominant stallion controls a herd of up to half-a-dozen mares and their foals. Stallions will fight viciously for control of his harem. Bachelor males either live alone or with groups of other bachelors until they are old enough to challenge a breeding stallion.

Young stallions can take over an established herd by defeating its controlling male in a violent contest of kicking and biting. Stallions are unable to breed until they have gained control of a herd. A herd's alpha male checks the reproductive condition of his mares by sniffing their urine.

The mares urinate more frequently as they come into heat and the male marks where they urinate. This deters potential rivals. When a zebra mare is on heat she presents herself to the stallion by standing with her hind legs splayed and her tail lifted to one side. The time taken to actually couple in mating is brief, but it is repeated every hour or so for two days.

A mare with a newborn foal is actively aggressive towards her herd companions. A foal is able to run beside its mother within an hour of birth. A mare is extremely possessive of her own foal, which she recognises by smell for a few days until she registers the pattern of its stripes. It takes 11 months before a foal is weaned. Zebras crossed with donkeys are known as 'zonkeys'.

# Tailpiece

**M**any people have had something to say about the human mating game, here are a few of my favourite aphorisms:

'Anybody who believes that the way to a man's heart is through his stomach flunked geography.' (Robert Byrne)

'Remember, if you smoke after sex you're doing it too fast.' (Woody Allen)

'Don't knock masturbation — it's sex with someone I love.' (Woody Allen)

'Life in Lubbock, Texas, taught me two things. One is that God loves you and you're going to burn in hell. The other is that sex is the most awful, filthy thing on earth and you should save it for someone you love.' (Butch Hancock)

'No matter how much cats fight, there always seem to be plenty of kittens.' (Abraham Lincoln)

'Familiarity breeds contempt – and children.' (Mark Twain, *Notebooks*, 1935)

'Love is the answer, but while you are waiting for the answer, sex raises some pretty good questions.' (Woody Allen)

'The natural man has only two primal passions: to get and beget.' (William Osler)

'Sex relieves tension – love causes it.' (Woody Allen)

'Sex is emotion in motion.' (Mae West)

'Whoever called it necking was a poor judge of anatomy.' (Groucho Marx)

'Why should we take advice on sex from the Pope? If he knows anything about it, he shouldn't!' (G B Shaw)

'For women the best aphrodisiacs are words. The G-spot is in the ears. He who looks for it below there is wasting his time.' (Isabel Allende)

'Sex without love is an empty experience. But as empty experiences go it's the best.' (Woody Allen)

'Sex between a man and a woman can be absolutely wonderful – provided you get between the right man and the right woman.' (Woody Allen)

'An intellectual is a person who's found one thing that's more interesting than sex.' (Aldous Huxley)

'I know nothing about sex, because I was always married.' (Zsa Zsa Gabor)

'Sex at age ninety is like trying to shoot pool with a rope.' (George Burns)

'The only thing wrong with being an atheist is that there's nobody to talk to during an orgasm.' (Anon)

'Men reach their sexual peak at eighteen. Women reach theirs at thirty-five. Do you get the feeling that God is playing a practical joke?' (Rita Rudner)

'Kids in back seats cause accidents. Accidents in back seats cause kids.' (Anon)

'Having sex is like playing bridge. If you don't have a good partner, you'd better have a good hand.' (Woody Allen)

'All lovers swear more performance than they are able.' (William Shakespeare)

'My father told me all about the birds and the bees, the liar – I went steady with a woodpecker till I was twenty-one.' (Bob Hope)

'Bisexuality immediately doubles your chances of a date on Saturday night.' (Woody Allen)

'I'm all for bringing back the birch, but only between consenting adults.' (Gore Vidal)

'The difference between light and hard is that you can sleep with a light on.' (Anon)

'I have an intense desire to return to the womb. Anybody's.' (Woody Allen)

'Kinky is using a feather. Perverted is using the whole chicken.' (Anon)

'When authorities warn you of the sinfulness of sex, there is an important lesson to be learned. Do not have sex with the authorities.' (Matt Groening)

'There are a number of mechanical devices which increase sexual arousal, particularly in women. Chief among these is the Mercedes-Benz 380SL convertible.' (P J O'Rourke)

'Love is not the dying moan of a distant violin – it's the triumphant twang of a bedspring.' (S J Perelman)

'I sold the memoirs of my sex life to a publisher. They are going to make a board game out of it.' (Woody Allen)

'If it weren't for pickpockets, I'd have no sex life at all.' (Rodney Dangerfield)

'Bigamy is having one husband or wife too many. Monogamy is the same.' (Oscar Wilde)

'During sex I sometimes fantasise that I'm somebody else.' (Richard Lewis)

'Sex is better than talk. Talk is what you suffer through so you can get to sex.' (Woody Allen)

'The prison psychiatrist asked me if I thought sex was dirty. I told him only when it's done right.' (Woody Allen)

'What are the three words you never want to hear while making love? "Honey, I'm home".' (Ken Hammond)

'I'm such a good lover because I practice so much on my own.' (Woody Allen)

'I've been too fucking busy. And vice versa.' (Dorothy Parker)

## BIRDS, BEES AND EDUCATED FLEAS

'Life is a sexually transmitted disease and the mortality rate is one hundred percent.' (R D Laing)

# Epilogue

When I began writing *Birds, Bees and Educated Fleas*, I intended it to be a light-hearted romp peeping at the sex lives of various animals. The bizarre mating habits of the barnacle and the lobster would, it seemed, set the tone of the tome.

I hadn't banked on doing so much research nor coming across so many sources that seemed to contradict each other. When unsure in whom to believe I turned to my trusty *Encyclopedia Britannica*, although even those volumes are not always comprehensive and quite a lot of information has had to be updated. (Other sources from which I have been able to tease out certain animal facts are listed at the end of this Epilogue.)

As I was barely halfway through my research and writing, I became increasingly aware of the devastating slaughter going on in the animal world, such as the senseless massacre of more than

100 elephants, killed by spreading cyanide on their salt licks in September 2013.

So, before putting the final manuscript in the hands of my editor at John Blake Publishing, Executive Editor Toby Buchan, I trawled through it and changed the tone a little by adding reminders of the poaching and slaughter going on. It is time the world sat up and took notice. With this in mind, I commend the reader to support the Duke of Cambridge's organisation, Tusk Force, which works to support conservation, education and community development across Africa. It encompasses a wide field of endeavour, not just elephants.

In a speech to mark Tusk's 20th anniversary, Prince William noted: 'The imperative of balancing conservation of wildlife and natural resources with the ever-growing needs of the human race is at the heart of the great challenge facing mankind today.'

Other organisations are rising to the challenge of conserving wildlife. One such is the George Adamson Wildlife Preservation Trust that was formed in 1979 to raise funds for the work being done in Kora National Park in northern Kenya. The Mkomazi National Park is a magnificent, 3,500 square kilometre game reserve. Remote and inaccessible, it was established in 1951, but never attracted the financial support provided for the better-known wildlife strongholds such as the Ngorongoro and the Serengeti National Parks. The George Adamson Wildlife Preservation Trusts have been the Tanzanian Government's main partner in this unique and important endeavour.

I am indebted to Dr Max Graham, the CEO of the Space for Giants organisation, a recently established charity designed to stop the illegal poaching of African elephants, for allowing me to quote from his Annual Report up until 2013:

'Our mission is to secure a future for the largest mammals on Earth forever, to be enjoyed by humanity forever, by ensuring they have the space and security to live and move freely in the wild, forever.

'It is increasingly evident that a solution is needed at the demand end of the market [for elephants] in Asia, particularly within China, if many elephant populations are to be spared imminent extinction. In addition the current scale of land-use change occurring in Africa in response to local economic growth and the global commodities boom has reduced the window for securing Africa's remaining elephant ranges and associated biodiversity. This makes our four programmes of work in Kenya all the more important for demonstrating models for conservation that can be rolled out into other critical elephant ranges.

'But it also means that we are going to have to broaden our horizons into new areas of work and new locations if we are going to achieve conservation success on a scale that is meaningful over the long term. It is for this reason that we have designed two new programmes, one for Africa and one for China.'

The Chairman of Space for Giants, Dr Boniface Kiteme, wrote: 'Not only is the threat of elephant poaching at an all-time high but we are also undergoing significant political and economic changes. Devolution of power to the counties, changes to land and wildlife policy and the implementation of the new constitution all present new opportunities and challenges for Space for Giant's work. So too does the new wave of massive infrastructure development projects that are set to transform the region forever.

'... the ultimate solution to the current elephant poaching crisis lies with the people of China and their leaders. To tackle this challenge Space for Giants will work in China to build awareness and change attitudes towards ivory consumption and African elephant conservation. You can help us to combat the ultimate cause of elephant poaching and habitat loss by investing in our China programme.

'Space for Giants is a small, focused and responsive conservation charity that is having a significant conservation impact on the ground. Our approach is highly collaborative and is informed by over 10 years of practical hands on applied research and conservation in Africa. We strongly believe we represent an ideal opportunity for donors looking for the best bang for their buck.'

UK residents wishing to make a donation to the charity should write a cheque to 'Space for Giants' and send it to: The Trustees, Space for Giants, 3 Danecroft Road, London, SE24 9PA. In the USA, cheques should be made payable to 'Tusk USA' and sent to: Tusk USA, 9 Village Lane, Santa Fe, NM 87505.

## SOURCE ATTRIBUTIONS
Attenborough, David, *The Trials of Life: A Natural History of Animal Behaviour*, (Collins/BBC, 1990)

*Behavioural Ecology and Sociobiology, Journal of*, published bi-monthly by the Oxford University Press
*Brewer's Dictionary of Phrase and Fable*, rev. Ivor J Evans (Cassell, 1981)

Brown, Augustus, *Why Pandas Do Handstands: and other curious truths about animals* (Bantam, 2006)

Defoe, Gideon, *How Animals Have Sex* (Weidenfeld & Nicolson, 2005)

Elphick, Jonathan, Green, Jen, Taylor, Barbara & Walker, Richard, *Encyclopedia of Animals* (Dorling Kindersley, 2000)

Mitchinson, John and Lloyd, John, *The Book of Animal Ignorance* (Faber & Faber, 2007)

*New Encyclopædia Britannica, The*, 15th edition, 29 volumes (Encyclopædia Britannica Inc, from 1974)

Spelma, Dr Lucy, *National Geographic Animal Encyclopedia* (National Geographic Society, 2012)

This is by no means a comprehensive list, and I would commend all Sir David Attenborough's books to the reader who really wants to take up the study of animal behaviour in any serious way.

And finally, I apologise if I have inadvertently perpetuated mischievous exaggerations that have grown like Chinese whispers over the years.

BRUCE MONTAGUE

Hove, June 2014